# Quiltopedia

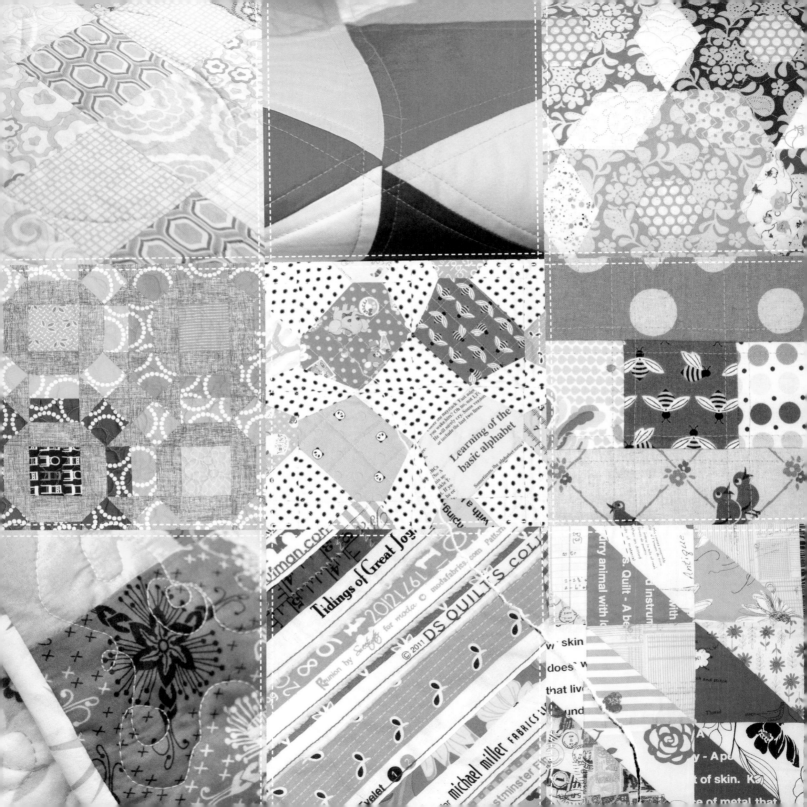

# Quiltopedia

The only quilting reference you'll ever need

**LAURA JANE TAYLOR**

**APPLE**

# Contents

A Quintet Book.
First published in the UK in 2014 by
Apple Press
74-77 White Lion Street,
London N1 9PF
United Kingdom

www.apple-press.com

ISBN: 978-1-84543-535-6
QTT:QUP

This book was conceived,
designed, and produced by
Quintet Publishing Limited
Sheridan House
114–116 Western Road
Hove BN3 1DD

Principal Photography: Lydia Evans
Additional Photography:
Laura Jane Taylor
Illustrator: Bernard Chau
Designer: Bonnie Bryan
Project Editor: Caroline Elliker
Technical Consultant: Fiona Calvert
Art Director: Michael Charles
Managing Editor: Emma Bastow
Publisher: Mark Searle

Manufactured in China by 1010
Printing International Ltd.

10 9 8 7 6 5 4 3 2 1

## Projects 100

# Introduction

# Introduction

The art of joining pieces of material together to form a quilt or blanket is an age-old tradition, but when you hear the term quilting, what do you think of? Does it connote quaint little English cottages and ditzy floral fabrics? Or perhaps civil war reproduction style prints and traditional block based designs? Maybe even harsh contrasts of bold colours and negative space?

## Early History

One of the earliest examples of a quilt (as we know them now) can be found at the V&A museum in London. It is the Tristan Quilt, a linen trapunto style quilt made in approximately 1360. However, the process of quilting pre-dates the Tristan Quilt by many centuries. Statues of Egyptian Pharaohs wearing quilted garments have been found dating back to approximately 3400 BCE.

Quilting would have originally started as a purely functional way of creating warm clothing; the process of layering the front, stuffing and back together traps air inside, which in turn warms the body. While there are these very early examples, quilting in general became more popular during the Middle Ages when Knights would wear them under armour and as protection from the elements.

During colonial times in America, the Europeans brought their quilts and quilt making skills with them. Quilting is a huge part of American history, in particular among the Amish. Amish quilts tend to favour a more traditional whole-cloth design rather than incorporating pieced elements.

Another huge step forward for quilting was with the invention of the home sewing machine in the mid 1800s. Suddenly, people were able to piece quickly and efficiently without having to stitch by hand. They could also devote more of their time to quilting for pleasure because their other sewing requirements could be achieved faster. Add to that the industrial revolution that was taking place at the time, making fabric much more affordable, and you can begin to see how quilting became commonplace in many homes.

Pictured here is my grandfather's Singer sewing machine, which he picked up for the princely sum of £5 from a charity shop in 1950. Using the identification number, I can trace its manufacturing date to 1891. And she still sews like a dream.

View of the back of a quilted white satin travelling petticoat c1745 from the Snowshill Collection at Berrington Hall, Leominster, UK.

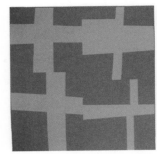

## Modern vs Traditional

What I love about quilting, from whichever style or tradition you approach it, is that you can take the techniques and make them your own. If you have a passion for paisley, go right ahead and make a paisley quilt. A lot of traditional quilt blocks will look amazing in different styles of fabric; choosing new fabrics to liven up an old pattern is one of my favourite things to do.

There has been great debate in recent years on the concept of modern versus traditional quilting. Modern quilts tend to focus on large swathes of bold colour, often playing on negative space and improvised styles and angles to achieve a strong look. They make use of a lot of solid fabrics, angular shapes, and graphical designs and layouts. Originally influenced by the works of the Gee's Bend quilters and Denyse Schmidt, the Modern Quilt Guild was formed in 2009 and is now a worldwide group of quilters all after that same fresh modern look.

For what it's worth, I consider myself a modern traditionalist. While I am not your average quilter, I believe that I am representative of a large group of new style quilters, those whose passion for the art is purely self-motivated and who treasure their traditional roots while searching for newer, more efficient ways to do things.

## Community

Quilting is so accessible these days with the popularity of the internet, blogs and social media websites. Quilters are a really friendly bunch, and all of the great things about the internet

and quilting can be summed up with the word 'community'. I feel the same level of community with my internet sewing besties (as I like to call them) as I expect the 1950s housewife did with the ladies on her street.

Virtual sewing bees, often run on photosharing websites such as Flickr, are a great way to form friendships and make quilts. I founded 'Brit Bee' in 2012; we are 12 girls from all over the UK who each month make a quilt for one member. See the Churn Dashing quilt on page 158 for an example, which was pieced by the 12 members of Brit Bee – thanks girls!

I would urge anyone taking up sewing and quilting to meet others doing the same. Find a local sewing group, hang out in your local quilt shop, or attend sewing retreats or guild meetings. Just get out there and have fun.

This book is a happy collaboration of all things quilty. A range of projects for different abilities will help you progress or extend your skills, while still building on the basics. Make up your own sampler quilt using the helpful block directory, and refer to the glossary and abbreviations at the back for further guidance. Quilting is a personal journey, and I'm thrilled to be leading the way for you.

May your rotary blade always be sharp, may your bobbin never run out in the middle of an 80-inch quilting line, and may your stash always contain that perfect shade of blue.

Happy stitching,

*Laura Jane Taylor*

Pictured here is the Four Crosses quilt by Denyse Schmidt, the queen of modern quilting. It is part of the Cotton Collection and is inspired by early Amish designs.

Churn Dashing quilt on page 158.

# Equipment

# & Materials

A good rotary cutter and ruler are the most important tools in a quilter's arsenal.

# Equipment

With the vast range of tools and equipment available for quilters these days, it can be a confusing hobby to get into. To begin, you really only need the basics: a good pair of scissors, a rotary cutter, a self-healing mat, a ruler and a seam ripper – the rest you can collect over time if necessary. Of course, unless you are planning to sew everything by hand, you will also need a sewing machine.

### Rotary Cutter

Generally available in three sizes; 60mm, 45mm, and 28mm, with the medium size being the most popular. They make cutting much quicker and easier than using scissors. Replacement blades can be bought at all good quilting shops.

### Rulers

All sorts of shapes and sizes of rulers are available. The ones I find most useful are the 6 x 24-inch (for cutting sashing strips, yardage, and anything the length of a FQ), the 12½-inch square (for squaring up blocks to the standard quilting block size and for cutting larger squares for piecing), and the 6½-inch square (for squaring up small blocks and cutting small pieces where a larger ruler is unnecessary).

### Cutting Mats

If I could only offer one piece of advice to new quilters it would be to buy the best and biggest cutting mat you can reasonably afford in terms of money and space. You will thank me later. A good self-healing cutting mat not only protects your surfaces, but it also prolongs the life of your rotary cutter blades. It is worth buying a reputable brand, and make sure it is marked in inches. Most quilting measurements are given in inches, so you will not make use of the features of the mat if you buy a centimetre square one.

### Die Cutters

An alternative or additional route to cutting patchwork shapes, the cutting machine works much like a mangle to squeeze the fabric on to the blades inside the dies as you roll it through the machine. These types of machines save a huge amount of time when cutting out for a quilt. They are always accurate, cut up to eight layers of fabric at once, and are really easy to use. I personally use the Sizzix Big Shot (pictured left) for the majority of my basic shapes.

The Sizzix Big Shot die cutter.

## Sewing Machine

Recommending which sewing machine to buy is somewhat outside the scope of this book. However, you do not need to spend a fortune to get started. Some of the more basic entry-level sewing machines will produce a nice stitch. On my 'must have' list of things to look for in a new sewing machine would be the following:

- Even and well spaced straight stitch.
- Ability to lower feed dogs for free motion quilting.
- Ability, integrated or otherwise, to use a walking/dual feed foot.
- Automatic needle threader and cutter.
- Large throat space.

The rest, i.e. 500+ decorative stitches, automatic buttonholes, cording feet etc, are all very nice and useful but somewhat superfluous for quilting. I sew on the Janome Horizon 7770, which in my opinion is a brilliant machine. It is definitely a good choice for quilters as it has an 11-inch throat space.

## Iron and Ironing Board

A good iron is crucial to getting perfectly flat patchwork pieces. Having tried irons from all price brackets, I still return to my trusty £45 one (Breville Power Steam 2200W). I like to press with a lot of steam, so I find a steam function invaluable. If you are short on space, a travel ironing board can be used; Ikea make a great fold-away mini ironing board. You could even make a small portable pressing pad by upholstering a wooden tray with some cotton batting and your favourite fabric.

## Scissors

While I use a rotary cutter for the majority of cutting tasks in my sewing room, I always need scissors for something. My favourite pair of scissors can be seen in the Travel Sewing Kit project (page 178). They are made by Olfa, have really good size handles, super sharp blades, and a really pointy tip. They are great for EPP (English Paper Piecing, page 58) and smaller hand projects. I also have a pair of dressmaking shears which have very long blades and are great for cutting yardage and for cutting out patterns; I like the multipurpose handle style of shears for comfort – as well as numerous pairs of generic fabric scissors and thread snips which are on hand in the sewing room. Whichever scissors you choose for quilting, make sure never to use them for paper as it blunts the blades much quicker than fabric, and always store them safely as they are very sharp.

You don't need to spend a lot of money to get a good steam iron for quilting.

Travel ironing boards still work great, and they take up less space in crowded sewing rooms.

A collection of scissors is useful for quilting – just don't use them to cut paper.

## Needles

Hand and machine sewing needles come in a variety of sizes suitable for different purposes. The packets are usually clearly marked with that purpose. In general, the heavier the fabric, the thicker needle you should use.

For hand sewing, needles mostly come in sizes 1 (being the thickest and longest) to 10 (being the thinnest and shortest). The most popular choices of needle are as follows:

**Sharps:** The most commonly used hand sewing needles, these are of medium length, have sharp tips and small rounded eyes, which will accommodate a standard thickness of thread.

**Embroidery:** These needles have a larger eye, and as such are easier to thread. They can be useful when hand quilting with thicker thread such as perle cotton.

**Quilting:** Generally shorter and thinner than most other needles, these are also known as 'betweens'. Their thinner construction helps them pass through multiple layers more easily.

**Machine Needles:** These are marked with two sizing conventions. The European sizes range from 60 to 120, and the American sizes from eight to 19. In both cases, the smaller the number the thinner the needle.

I have found Superior Top stitch needles in size 80/12 to be the best all-round needle for piecing, sewing items such as bags and pouches, and for top stitching. They are titanium-coated and last considerably longer than any other needles that I have tried. They have a very sharp point and so can be used on a multitude of fabrics with great success. For quilting, I generally use Schmetz 75/11 needles, which have slightly longer, more tapered points and stronger shafts.

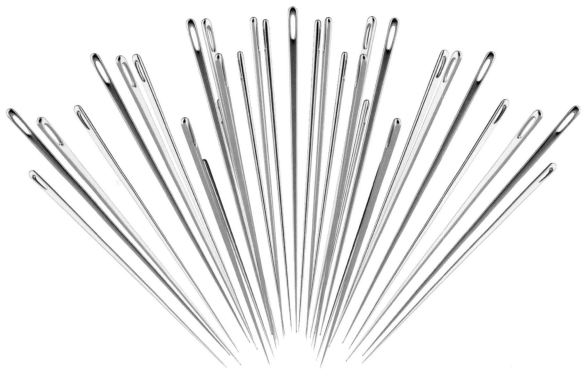

Machine needles always have one flattened side at the base of the needle; this usually needs to be located at the back when inserting into the machine.

## Needle size to fabric weight

| European/American | Fabric Weight |
| --- | --- |
| 60/8 | Very light |
| 65/9 | Light |
| 70/10 | Light |
| 75/11 | Light |
| 80/12 | Medium |
| 90/14 | Medium |
| 100/16 | Heavy |
| 110/18 | Very Heavy |
| 120/20 | Very Heavy |

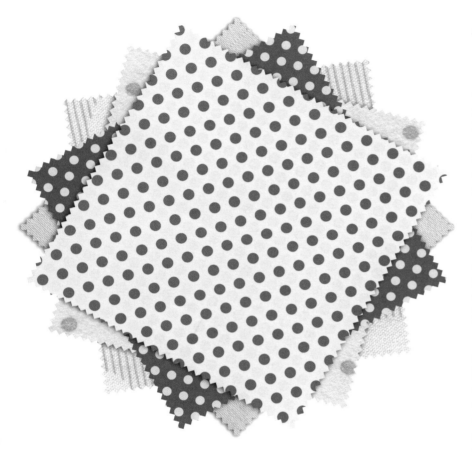

# Materials

### Choosing and Buying Fabric

Stash building is one of quilters' favourite pastimes. Really it is just shopping for fabric, but we take it very seriously. Having a 'well balanced stash' is an aim of most quilters – being able to walk up to your fabric storage and find you have the perfect fabric for a new project. This, of course, means shopping!

When building your stash, try to visualise what you own already and shop for any holes. Holes will naturally occur as, a) we gravitate towards our favourite colours and, b) the fabrics that are produced tend to be heavily weighted in favour of some colours more than others. I guarantee that if you look at any quilter's stash they will have more blues and greens than anything else.

Combining fabrics and choosing colours for a quilt is a fine art. Personally, I think that if you throw enough different fabrics into the mix, it has no option but to turn out well. Think of all the scrappy quilts you've ever seen – all those tiny pieces, chosen at random and pieced together, seemingly without consideration, to create a beautiful, colourful masterpiece. However, if you are working to a specific brief or with a smaller stash, or you just want to create a specific theme of quilt, here are some helpful tips for choosing fabrics.

## Colour Wheel

The colour wheel is a great place to start for inspiration. Think back to your school lessons on colour to help you choose fabrics for your quilt.

**Primary colours** are red, yellow and blue.

**Secondary colours** are made by mixing any two of the three primary colours to make orange, purple and green.

**Tertiary colours** are made by mixing any two primary and secondary colours to get red–orange, orange–yellow, yellow–green, blue–green, blue–violet and violet–red.

**High contrast colours** are any colours that are opposite each other on the colour wheel – i.e. green and red or blue and orange are known as high contrast or complementary colours. These can be great to create stark differences and very defined areas in your quilts.

**Harmonising colours** are any three colours that sit next to each other on the colour wheel, such as orange, yellow and red. These will create a blended effect in your quilt and will be pleasing to the eye.

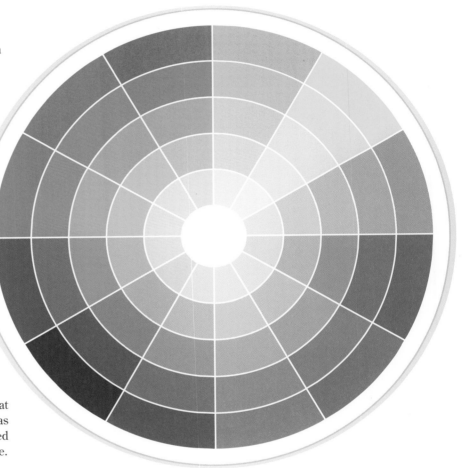

There is a wealth of information available on the internet about basic colour theory, as well as online tools to help you pick a palette. My favourites are:

**Design Seeds; http://design-seeds.com** – a huge database of photographs where the accent colours have been pulled out to the side like paint samplers.

**Colr; http://www.colr.org** and **DeGraeve; http://www.degraeve.com/color-palette/** are both brilliant sites for uploading your own picture and choosing a palette from that.

Notice how the shapes of the pieces in this block are all exactly the same, but the light and dark values create the pattern.

## Value

Value is important to consider when choosing fabrics for a quilt. The value of a fabric relates to how light or dark it is. It is nothing to do with the actual shade of colour, just its brightness. A great way of testing whether you have the value mix right or whether a particular composition looks correct is to remove all colour, i.e. take a black and white photo. When viewing the fabrics in grey scale, you can really tell how light or dark they are and whether you need more or less contrast.

## Theme

Designing a quilt based on a theme is a tricky subject. You want to highlight the essence of the theme without it looking too forced. Some popular themes you may want to use in your work are:

- Japanese.
- Text prints.
- Low value background.
- Rainbow colours.
- Linen and bright colours.
- Linen and bright colours.

In this textile fish, each tiny piece of fabric is cut out, stitched down to a base and then layered and quilted. Quilt art such as this is generally not much thinner than traditional quilting.

### Types of Fabric

As a newcomer to the quilting world, it is easy to be overwhelmed by the fabric choices. A good rule of thumb when you start out is to use 100 per cent cotton quilting weight fabric. That way, all your fabrics will be the same weight. You can then think about branching out into new fabric choices when you are comfortable with the basic processes.

In the US, fabric is sold by the yard. In the UK, Europe and Australia, it is sold by the metre. Most patterns are written in imperial units (including those in this book), so do check you are buying the correct amount for your pattern. The most common measurement of fabric that quilters buy is a 'fat quarter'. This is a quarter of a yard, and the yard is cut into four equal fat rectangles. This is different from a long quarter, which is a quarter of a yard from selvedge to selvedge.

Quilters find this type of fat cut gives them more usable fabric. Fat quarters are a great way to build up variation in your stash. They are affordable and often pre-cut in a store, so you don't need to take yardage up to the cutting desk. Fabric can also be bought in smaller increments such as fat eighths or even fat sixteenths, but this is less common.

Fabric, much like with fashion, is designed in a collection or line. The designers create anywhere from six to 40 prints that co-ordinate and complement each other on many levels. The basic elements of a fabric line include:

**Feature Prints:** large scale or complex prints, a bright, focal point of the line.

**Mid Prints:** medium scale, medium complexity prints. Often if the focal print is geometric, the mid prints will be floral and vice versa.

**Basic/Blender Prints:** essential simplified prints to bulk out the collection. Think polka dots, stripes, small scale floral, etc.

Pre-cut selections of fabric help you get a good variety of prints all at once.

Balance is the feature of any fabric collection. It is a cohesive mix of values, colour, scale and tone. When starting out, working with one collection is a great idea because you don't have to worry about all the above for your quilt. You can grab a fabric line and get sewing. A great way of buying fabrics in a complete collection is with pre-cuts. The most commonly available pre-cuts come in the form of:

**Jelly Rolls:** 42 x 2½ inches x WOF strips; use for strip twist quilts, triangles, rail fence, etc.

**Layer Cakes:** 42 x 10-inch squares; large scale patchwork, HSTs, QSTs, snowballs, etc.

**Charm Packs:** 42 x 5-inch squares; great for baby quilts, swaps, making HSTs, etc.

Of course, as you become more familiar with your fabric likes and dislikes, you might not want to use all the prints from one collection. In fact, many experienced quilters will mix their favourite prints from multiple lines and create what is known as a fabric pull. This is similar to creating a fabric bundle or line, but you are working with what you have in your stash to create a mix of fabrics for a particular project.

Many modern quilters buy their fabric from online stores for a number of reasons; the price is often lower and the variety greater, plus you don't actually have to leave the house to buy it. However, nothing beats seeing, touching and comparing fabric in person. If you are lucky to have a LQS (local quilting store) near to you, it would definitely be worth a visit.

A jelly roll featuring prints from Oh Deer! by Momo for Moda.

The different substrates, or base cloths, available for quilting are as follows:

### Quilting Weight Cotton

A light to mid weight 100 per cent cotton fabric designed for quilting. Usually printed on only one side, it has a definite right and wrong side. Available at local quilting shops, online shops, department stores and craft shops.

### Organic Quilting Cotton

Similar to the above. The organic quilting weight cotton market has grown substantially in recent years. Manufacturers such as Cloud9 and Birch use only organic base cloth, and most other manufacturers carry a line or two. The differences between organic and normal quilting weight cotton are slight; organic is a subtly lighter weight fabric with a slightly silkier feel.

Natural cotton quilts are lightweight and perfect for summer.

### Batik

Colourful fabrics dyed/printed using a traditional wax resist technique. The fabric has a stiffer hand because of the intensive dyeing process.

### Muslin (US)/Calico (UK)

Un-dyed, natural fabric that is the same weight as quilting cotton. It can be used as a foundation for FPP or as backing for appliqué blocks. This is not to be confused with cheesecloth (US)/muslin (UK) which is a much lighter and looser weave used for straining jam, for example.

### Vintage Sheets

These have become very popular recently due to the thrifting movement and 'make do and mend' ethos – a very cost effective way of backing a quilt. These sheets are available in a range of vintage patterns, some more attractive than others. They are often made from a polycotton mix, so pay attention to pressing and washing instructions.

### Linen

This is a heavier weight and looser weave fabric than quilting cotton, but they are often paired together for a sleek and modern look. It is available natural as well as dyed but frays easily. Linen is popular but less than ideal for quilting, so fabric manufacturers produce a range of linen-mix and linen-look fabrics, as well as other textured basics. The linen-mix fabrics are a 55/45 blend with cotton, so the fabric retains the strength of the linen but with more of the versatility of quilting weight cotton. The linen-look fabrics are the same base cloth as quilting weight cotton, but they are printed with a linen or canvas texture.

Quilt made entirely out of polyester material from the 1970s.

### Solids

Solid fabrics are useful to modern quilters for adding an extra dimension to patterns. They create visual contrast with the prints and give the eye a place to rest. All solid quilts are a work of art in themselves, often paired with an improvised style of piecing to create a dramatic modern look. Solids have no right or wrong side and are the same quality base cloth as quilting weight cotton. Colour cards are available for the most popular lines of solids (Kona Cotton, Bella Solids, Couture Solids), which quilters can use to match a solid to a particular print.

### Shot Cottons

Similar to solids in that they are not printed but woven, shot cottons have no right or wrong side. They are made by using different coloured threads for the weft and warp, which give the appearance of iridescence when the fabric catches the light in different ways.

### Voile

A silky smooth and lightweight fabric, voile is usually used in dress making. Fabric designers and manufacturers have started to produce more of their designs on voile and other substrates due to increased demand in the quilting industry. Voile is luxurious, buttery soft, and quilts up beautifully.

### Corduroy/Velveteen

A rich and heavy weight, corduroy is an 'up and coming' cotton substrate in the quilting world. It is traditionally used for garment sewing, but as more prints are being produced on this substrate, more quilters are using it. Corduroy often has an added percentage of spandex, so the grain and stretch must be paid particular attention when sewing a complex quilt pattern. Velveteen has a distinctive nap which can hinder the piecing process. A ½-inch seam allowance is advised with both.

### Flannel

A brushed cotton heavier weight fabric, flannel is traditionally used for winter garments and PJs as well as for backing quilts. Pre-washing is advised with flannel as it can shrink up to five per cent. A ½-inch seam allowance is advised.

### Oilcloth or Coated/Laminated Cotton

Oilcloth, or coated/laminated cotton, is a wipe-clean type of fabric. It comes in differing weights; anything from shower-curtain type material, right up to thick table-cloth plastic. Oilcloth can be sewn on a regular sewing machine with a Teflon foot. It is really useful for lining toiletry bags, and for the bases of tote bags. A lot of fabric designers will produce one or two laminate prints to complement their collection, usually in a slightly larger scale print or in a slightly different colourway.

Shot cottons are woven with two different coloured threats to give a subtle iridescence to the resulting fabric.

## Types of Wadding/Batting

When choosing a batting for your quilt or small project, it is good to keep its purpose in mind. The key measurement with batting is loft. This relates to how thick, airy and fluffy the batting is. For projects that will always want to lie flat – such as wall hangings and table runners – a low loft batting will give the best results. For a comfy snuggly quilt, a higher loft batting could be used. High loft battings are harder to quilt than low loft battings, either by hand or machine.

### Cotton

100 per cent cotton batting gives a very soft, drapey look to finished quilts. It is generally very flat, so it is low loft. Cotton will shrink when washed, which will give your quilt that lovely antique crinkly look. If that isn't the style you prefer, you will need to pre-wash the batting. Because of the way the cotton fibres are manufactured, pure cotton batting may require closer quilting than the equivalent synthetic blend. Always read the manufacturer's directions before starting so that you can plan and space accordingly. Cotton batting is available in a range of shades from bleached pure white, many shades of natural, dark grey, and even black.

### Cotton/Synthetic Blend

There are many cotton blend battings available, and the most popular is 80/20 cotton/polyester. These are great multi-purpose battings that retain the drape and feel of cotton but with the added strength of the synthetic fibre. They often require less quilting – you can leave greater spaces un-quilted without the batting bunching or shifting

While synthetic batting is often more widely available, it is worth searching out a cotton or cotton blend if you can.

over time. This is good for beginners and people who aren't so fond of the densely quilted look. The removal of some of the cotton content causes them to be lighter in weight, so they may be more suitable for large quilts.

### Bamboo

Probably the softest and silkiest of all the battings, bamboo has incredible characteristics in fabric. It dries three times faster than cotton and is much lighter in weight. For this reason, it may be a good choice for larger bed quilts. It is very low loft, so it is easy on the hands for hand quilting.

### Wool

Wool is the warmest and snuggliest type of batting available – suitable for a winter quilt. It can be hard on the hands for quilting because of the thickness of the material. Wool blends are also available, with cotton and polyester being the most popular secondary fibre. If you are considering wool, a blend might be a good option because they are lighter and easier to work with.

### Synthetic

Synthetic batting is often what people think of when they begin quilting. It is usually available in three thicknesses, ranging from high loft to very high loft. Because of its squishy texture, every step of the process is more difficult. The layers are harder to secure together for basting, it is cumbersome when handling and trying to fit through a domestic machine, and it is hard on the hands for hand quilting.

**Tip**
Excess batting is great for collecting dust or snips of thread. Pin a little to your shoulder when working to catch cast-offs and avoid a messy sewing room floor.

## Types of Backing Fabrics

The options for backing a quilt are almost as wide and varied as the options for the front fabrics. Which one you choose is down to personal choice and based on the look you want to create, the price of the fabric and the intended purpose of the quilt.

Remember that if your quilt is larger than 42 inches wide, you will need to piece the back from two lengths of fabric. Work out how much backing fabric you need:

**Step One** Find length of quilt in yards, eg. a 60 x 70-inch quilt is just under two yards in length.

**Step Two** If width of quilt is wider than 42 inches, then double the yard figure above, eg. four yards.

**Step Three** Add an extra ¼ yard for your sanity, eg. 4¼ yards.

**Step Four** Fold the fabric so that raw edges meet and cut in half along the fold.

**Step Five** Sew together down the selvedge side.

### Standard Quilting Cotton

If it's good enough for the front, it's certainly good enough for the back. Backing a quilt in quilting weight cotton is a great way to use prints that may have too large a scale to be used in your patchwork. If you are working with one line of fabric, you could choose one print to feature on the back, or you could go for a complete contrast. Piecing the quilt back from multiple fabrics – although more time consuming – gives the quilt some extra flair. It can be a good way to use up orphan blocks or leftover pieces.

### Corduroy/Flannel/Voile

Different substrates will give a luxurious feel to a special quilt. Voile and flannel are particularly good for baby quilts as they are softer and more tactile than quilting weight cotton. Voile can be used to back a lighter summer quilt, while corduroy and flannel are warm, snuggly, and great for heavier winter quilts.

### Fleece/Cuddle Fur

Fleece is an option for children's quilts and blankets. With these thicker weight fabrics you may decide to forgo the batting layer and quilt directly on to the fleece/minky or use the bagging out method of quilt construction.

### Extra Wides

This is quilting weight cotton that is 108 inches wide. This tends to be the maximum size of any quilt, so long-arm quilting machines are limited to this size. Extra wides are great when you are in a hurry and don't want to piece the back of your quilt. They may seem expensive at face value, but considering the fabric is three yards wide, they are actually very cost effective. The fabric itself is often slightly lighter weight than quilting weight cotton. Traditionally, extra wides only come in the most basic of shades and patterns, but more and more modern designs are being produced.

### Bed Sheets

This is a very cost and time effective way of finishing a quilt. Duvet covers can be unpicked at the side seams, and sheets can be used. Be aware of the fibre content and washing instructions for the sheet, as most are usually a polycotton mix. It is advisable to pre-wash before using to check for colour fastness and shrinkage.

One of my favourite quilt backings, as you will see on the Obsession Quilt, page 148, is from Ikea. Always be on the look out, even in unusual places, for quilt backing fabric.

**Tip**
You can pick up great deals on quilting weight cotton in the sale section of any shop – these discounts make for great cheap backings.

## Thread

Thread is manufactured in different weights; the smaller the number, the thicker the thread. A good quality 50wt cotton thread is the best choice for beginners because it can be used for all quilting steps.

**50wt** is a great multi-purpose thread used for piecing, hand sewing, and quilting where the quilting lines should sink into the background.

**40wt** is a slightly thicker thread, again multi-purpose, but if used for quilting the lines will show somewhat more.

**30wt** is a thicker thread used where emphasis on the thread is needed. Good for decorative top stitching and heavy quilting.

**12wt** is a very thick thread used mostly for decorative purposes.

**8wt or 5wt** is a chunky weight thread akin to embroidery floss, which can be used for hand quilting or decorative purposes.

Try a few different thread manufacturers and thicknesses until you find one that works well for you. All of the projects in this book (with the exception of the hand quilting) have been pieced and quilted with Aurifil thread in either 50wt or 40wt. Through a lot of trial and error, I have decided that Aurifil threads are my favourite.

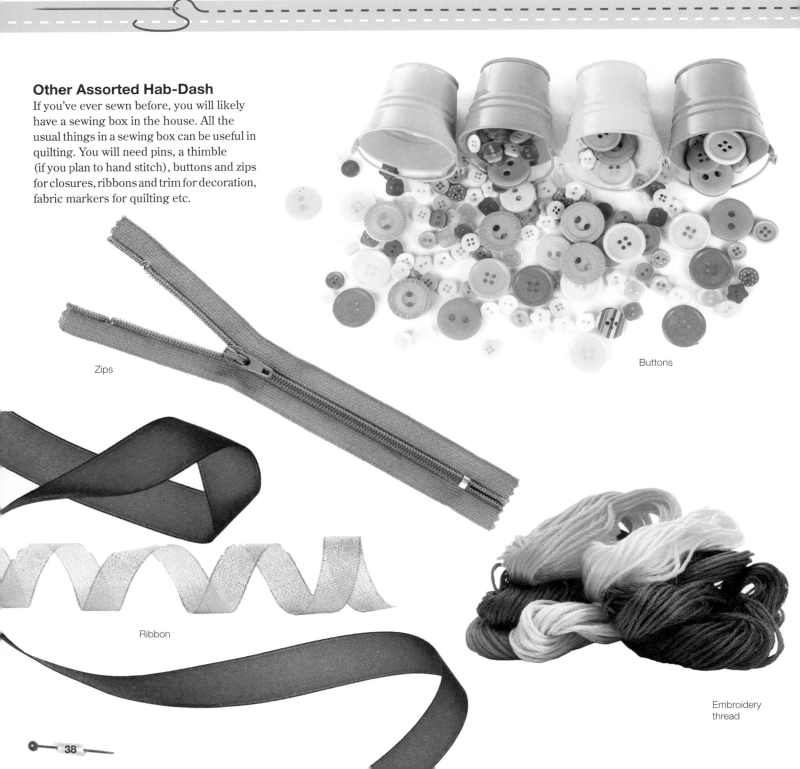

## Other Assorted Hab-Dash

If you've ever sewn before, you will likely have a sewing box in the house. All the usual things in a sewing box can be useful in quilting. You will need pins, a thimble (if you plan to hand stitch), buttons and zips for closures, ribbons and trim for decoration, fabric markers for quilting etc.

Buttons

Zips

Ribbon

Embroidery thread

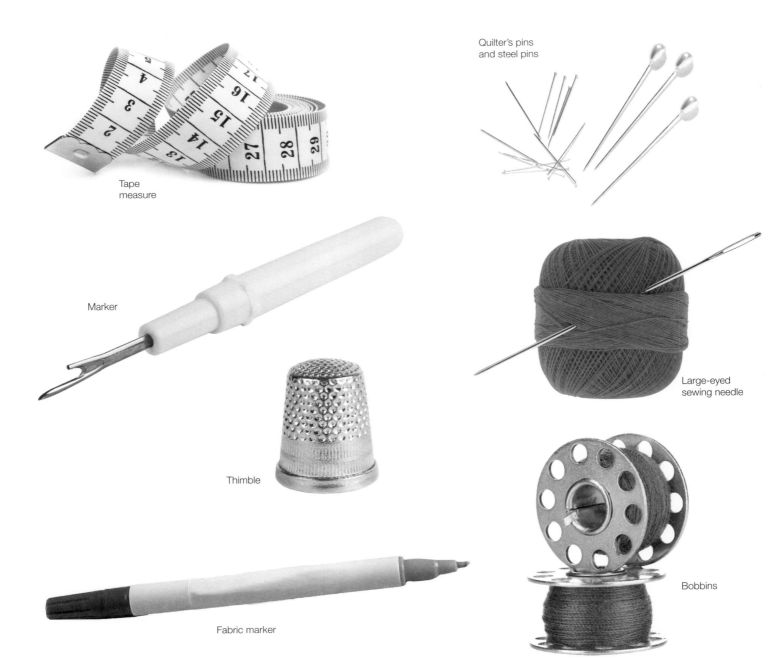

Tape
measure

Quilter's pins
and steel pins

Marker

Large-eyed
sewing needle

Thimble

Bobbins

Fabric marker

39

# Techniques

# Techniques

These are the foundation techniques you need when learning how to quilt. Once you have mastered these skills, you will be able to pick up any fabric and create beautiful patchwork quilts.

## Rotary Cutting

Learning to be comfortable with a rotary cutter will be the single biggest time saver in your quilting endeavours. They are quick, accurate and powerful. Rotary blades can easily cut through six layers of fabric at once without losing any degree of accuracy. Rotary blades are very sharp when new, so be mindful of yourself and your surroundings. All good brands of rotary cutters have auto retract options on the blade.

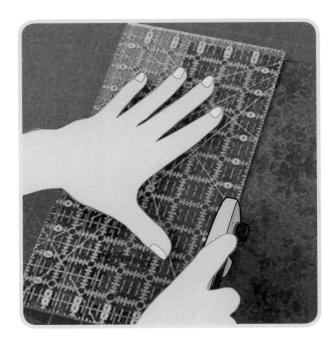

**1** Lay the ironed fabric on your cutting mat, aligning the selvedge with one of the lines on the mat. This makes sure you are cutting straight and on the grain.

**2** Lay the ruler covering the area to be cut, apply pressure to the ruler to prevent it from slipping, and trim the edges of the fabric. The rotary blade should run up the side of the ruler, not drift off away from it.

**3** Continue turning and cutting until the piece is the size you require. To cut pieces that are larger than your fabric or ruler, you will need to fold the fabric first.

## Cutting Equilateral Triangles

Equilateral triangles have the same length sides and same 60-degree angle in each of their three corners.

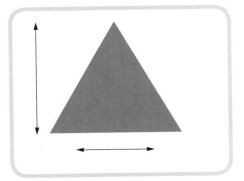

**1** Decide on the finished size of your triangles. Add ½ inch to that measurement and cut a fabric strip of that width x WOF.

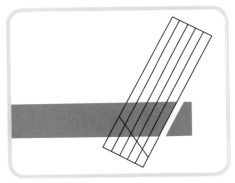

**2** Align the 60-degree line on your ruler with the long edge of the strip.

**3** Cut along the right edge of the ruler to trim the fabric to a 60-degree edge. This will start your row of triangles.

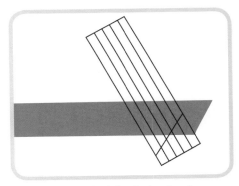

**4** Swing ruler to the left, aligning its other 60-degree line along the bottom edge of the strip. Position the edge of the ruler to form the 'point' at the bottom edge of your first cut.

**5** Cut along the right side of the ruler to create a triangle.

**6** Continue swinging your ruler left and right to cut more triangles.

## Piecing an Accurate Seam

For quilting, most seams are sewn at ¼ inch. Accuracy is essential, or patchwork pieces will not match up with each other properly when it's time to sew components together.

A ¼-inch foot will be invaluable to you when you start quilting. There is a little metal guide that runs along the side of it to keep the fabric perfectly in line. If your machine did not come with one, I heartily recommend investing in one. You will not regret it.

If you are using a non-standard fabric, such as voile or flannel, something that will fray easily, or something that requires more strength in the seam, you may be advised to use ⅜ inch. If you are sewing something requiring a greater degree of precision, you may be required to use a scant ¼-inch seam. Always read the instructions in the pattern; they will usually assume ¼ inch if not stated.

### To check your seams are coming out at a perfect ¼-inch

**1** Cut three strips of fabric, 1½ x 4 inches.

**2** Join all three fabrics along the 4-inch side using your ¼-inch foot.

**3** Finger press the two edge pieces away from the centre.

**4** Measure the width of the centre strip. It should measure exactly 1 inch. If it does not, adjust your needle position to the left or right to cater for the difference.

## Chain Piecing

Chain piecing is a time saving process – it means you do not cut the thread in between sewing patchwork shapes together.

**1** Pair the two patchwork pieces to be sewn, RST. When you finish sewing the piece, do not cut thread.

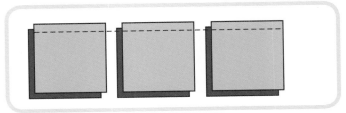

**2** Bring the next pair up to the sewing machine and continue sewing. Repeat for however many pieces there are to your block.

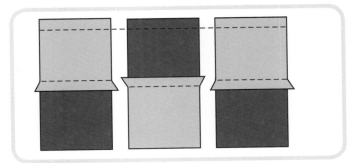

**3** Press all seams in alternate directions and clip the threads between the pieces.

## Pressing

Pressing is required in every step of making a patchwork quilt. It is important to note that this is not the same as ironing. When pressing, the hot iron should be applied to the fabric in an up-and-down motion, rather than side-to-side. This is to avoid the seams being stretched out of shape.

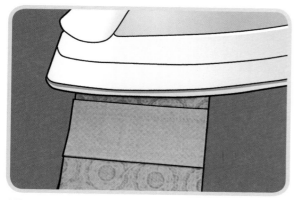

1 Take pieced unit to ironing board and press while it is still folded RST. This is known as 'setting the seam'.

2 When cooled, flip open the pieced unit and press it so it lays flat.

### There are two main methods of pressing seams:

**Open**

Each half of the seam is folded back on itself. This is useful for lighter coloured fabrics and to reduce bulk in complex points.

**To the Side**

Both halves of the seam are pressed to the dark side of the block. This is useful for nesting seams when joining blocks.

Tip

It is entirely a personal choice as to how you press your seams. I like to nest seams when chain piecing and I like the extra security of two layers of fabric rather than an open seam, so unless otherwise directed by a pattern I always press my seams to the side.

## Squaring Up

In order to maintain accuracy in your quilt – and to help ease the blocks together into their finished layouts – most quilt blocks will need to be squared up. This is particularly important with blocks such as half-square triangles because they are purposefully sewn larger than necessary and then trimmed back.

You will need a square ruler, preferably one with a diagonal line running across it. I like 12½-inch square rulers because they can be used even on larger squares. Also, you may find a rotating cutting mat useful, but it is not necessary.

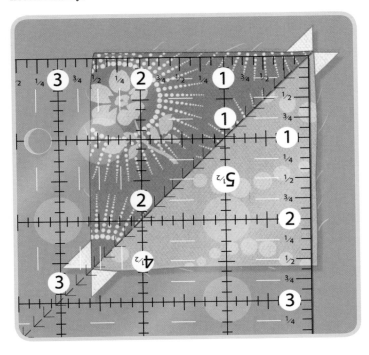

1 Begin by laying your ruler on top of the block with the numbers counting up from the top right to the top left. If your block has a diagonal line running through the centre, like with a half-square triangle, be sure to align that with the diagonal line on the ruler. If it does not, simply align the top right and bottom left points with the diagonal line of the ruler.

2 Make sure that the line for the size of block you wish to cut, in this case 2½ inches, is covered all the way around the shape. Trim the right hand side and the top of the block.

3 Remove the ruler, rotate the block through 180 degrees, and align the 2½-inch (in this case) line with the edges you cut in step two. Now trim the right hand side and top of the block again.

## Basic Block Construction

The majority of quilt blocks are based on the idea of a grid. How many patches you need will depend on how many rows and columns are in that grid. For example, a four-patch layout is four squares, sewn together to make one larger square in a two by two layout. A nine- or 16-patch is the same, but in three by three or four by four layouts.

Basic patchwork quilts, made entirely from squares, are still one of my favourites. They have a timeless quality and really let the fabrics sing.

**1** Arrange squares in desired layout.

**2** Sew into rows.

**3** Press, alternating directions of seams.

**4** Pair rows, nest seams, join.

**5** Press final seams open (I like to do this to reduce bulk in the points, but it is not absolutely necessary).

Mixing squares and HSTs (half-square triangles) yields endless possibilities for quilt patterns.

## Half-Square Triangles

Half-square triangles (HSTs) are one of the most versatile and most used shapes in patchwork and quilting. You can create so many quilt designs using just this humble shape.

**1** Decide on the size for your squares by adding ⅞ inch to your finished size. If you want 3-inch finished HSTs, cut your squares at 3⅞ inches. TIP: Cut your squares a full 1 inch larger if you are unsure about the scantness of your seams. It will mean you have more to trim, but will give you a more accurate sized block.

**2** Draw a diagonal line down the centre of one of the squares.

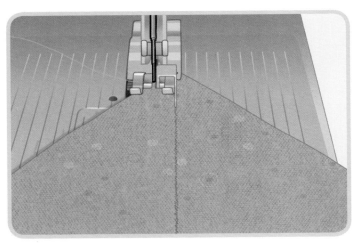

**3** Pair squares, RST, and sew a scant ¼-inch either side of the line.

**4** Cut on the drawn line to yield two HST units.

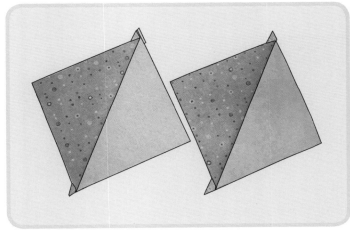

**5** Press and square up to desired size, making sure to trim off the extra bits at the edges. These are known as doggy ears.

Use contrasting value fabrics for each half of the HST to create new patterns from the basic shapes.

## Quarter-Square Triangles

Quarter-square triangles (QSTs) occur when two HSTs are joined together. They are also known as hourglass, or spool blocks, and create a cute pattern when sewn up in contrasting colours.

**1** Decide on the size for your squares by adding 1½ inches to your finished size. If you want 3-inch finished QSTs, cut your squares at 4½ inches.

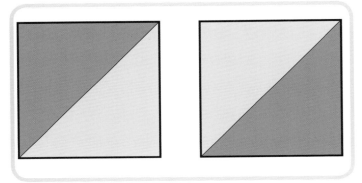

**2** Make HSTs from these two squares following steps two–five of the HST instructions.

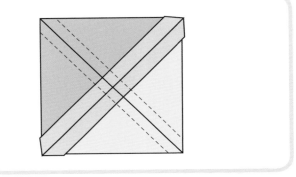

**3** Draw a diagonal line on the reverse side of one of the HSTs, running perpendicular to the previously sewn line. Pair HSTs and sew a scant ¼-inch either side of the line.

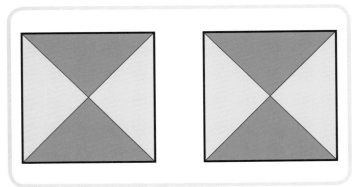

**4** Cut on the line to yield two QST units.

**5** Press and square up to desired size, making sure to trim the doggy ears.

The Happy Picnic Table
Runner on page 134 gives
the effect of QSTs using a
different sewing technique.

## Corner-Square Triangles

Corner-square triangles (CSTs) are useful for rounding off corners, creating octagons from squares, and for setting blocks on-point. This is also known as the stitch and flip technique.

Snowball blocks are one of my favourites to make a quick and easy baby quilt. See Snowball Block in Block Directory on page 204.

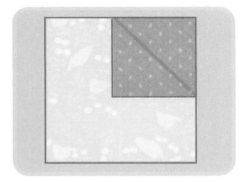

**1** Draw a diagonal line across a small square.

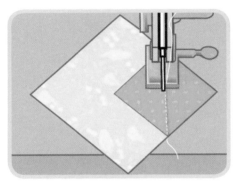

**2** Place RST with large square so that the drawn line goes across the corner, not to the corner point.

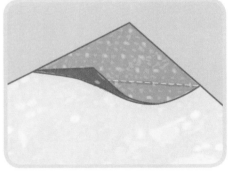

**3** Sew across the line.

**4** Trim excess fabric ¼ inch from sewn line.

**5** Flip triangle over and press.

**Tip**

Sew a second line in step three, ½ inch closer to the corner than the first. When you trim the excess in step four, you will be cutting between two sewn lines, this will create a bonus HST from your scraps. If you are doing a project with lots of CSTs you may be able to make a second project with the leftover HSTs.

## Flying Geese

Flying geese are another staple quilting block. They can be put together to make larger groups or flocks of geese, and are often used as borders.

Foundation paper piecing can also be used to create flying geese in more complex arrangements.

**1** Draw a diagonal line across two small squares. Align the first square with the right hand corner of the rectangle. Sew across diagonal line.

**3** Press triangle over to create rectangle shape.

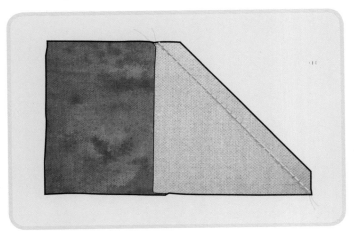

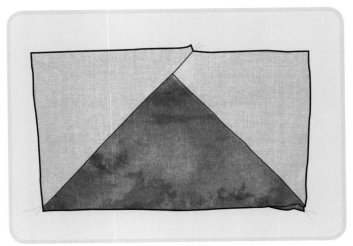

**2** Trim excess fabric ¼ inch from sewn line.

**4** Repeat for the second corner.

## Partial Seams

Some quilt blocks are designed to 'pinwheel' around a central design. These are like log cabin blocks, but there is no clear beginning to the round. Partial seams are actually very easy to master and can give an extra dimension of complexity to your sewing.

**1** Sew first log, RST to the central patch. Sew only half way along the seam.

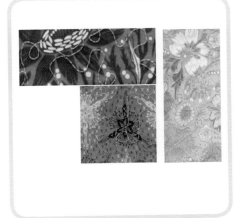

**2** Add the following log in the same way you normally would with a log cabin, sewing the whole seam as usual.

**3** Add the third log in the same way you normally would, sewing the whole seam as usual.

**4** Flip the first log out of the way, and sew the fourth log as usual.

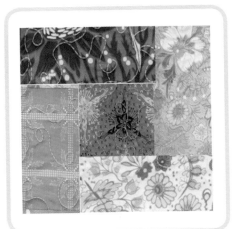

**5** Align the first log with the last log, and finish the rest of the seam.

## English Paper Piecing

English paper piecing (EPP) is the age-old method of basting fabric on to paper shapes and then sewing them together. This work is done by hand. It is useful for shapes that are more difficult to sew, such as hexagons, because you don't need to worry about partial seams.

**1** Lay paper shape on top of fabric and trim seam allowance to ¼ inch and no smaller. You can hold the paper piece in place with a dab of glue or pin at this stage (optional).

**2** Thread your needle with approximately 18 inches of cotton thread and knot the end.

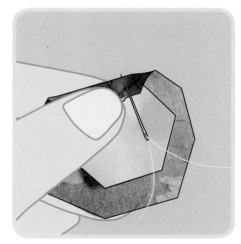

**3** Fold over the first edge and make a nice tight fold. Take your threaded needle and make one stitch through the fabric and paper, approximately ¼ inch in from the edge. Start this stitch from the wrong side.

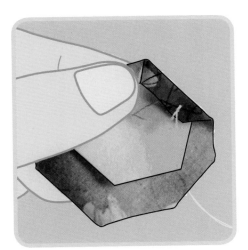

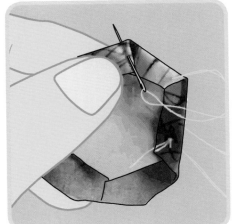

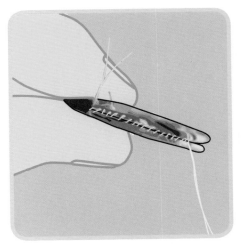

**4** Make a second fold on the next corner clockwise around the shape. Make sure to be tight and neat around the corner area.

**5** Bring needle through from the back (right side) of the shape. With this stitch, you are securing the first folded side, the first corner and the second folded side all at once.

**6** Make the second corner by folding over the third side and securing. Stitch through this corner once, from front (wrong side) to back.

**7** Repeat for the rest of the shape until all corners are basted. There is no need to secure threads when you reach the last corner – just leave a long tail.

**8** When all shapes are basted, join. I find it easiest to work in rows when completing a large EPP project. To join, hold two shapes RST, and make a stitch exactly in the corner.

**9** Continue whip stitching the shapes together, making only very small stitches and only catching the fabric, not the paper.

**10** When all shapes are joined, press, remove basting stitches and papers, and use as desired. You can either appliqué the shapes on to a background, or use them in your projects as a standard patchwork piece of fabric.

## Tip

There are so many resources available for EPP:

**http://incompetech.com/graphpaper** Design and print your own paper templates.

**http://www.paperpieces.com/** An online shop to buy paper pieces. They have a huge range of shapes available from hexagons to double wedding ring designs.

## Foundation Paper Piecing

Foundation paper piecing (FPP) is used by quilters to create complex shapes that would otherwise be difficult to cut and sew together, perhaps due to many small pieces or odd angles. The fabric is sewn directly on to a printed piece of paper, following printed lines. Wrapping your head around the concept of FPP is tricky to begin with as you are, in effect, working a backwards mirror image, but once you've understood the basics it can be a great tool to have under your belt.

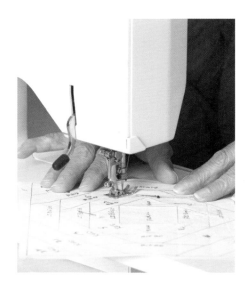

1 Print pattern out on plain paper. Ensure your printer is set to 'no scaling' so the pattern prints out at the correct size.

2 Some people like to pre-perforate their pattern to make the paper easier to tear and so that they can see the sewing lines on both sides of the paper. To do this, unthread your sewing machine and sew over all the lines.

3 Take your first fabric piece – this should be cut at least ¼ inch larger than the shape all the way round. I like to cut at ½ inch larger for more breathing room. You will trim later. Hold the piece against the reverse of the pattern, up to the light, so that you can see it covers the whole area. Take the second piece and place RST with the first so that when the seam is sewn and the piece is flipped over, it will cover the second segment. Pin in place.

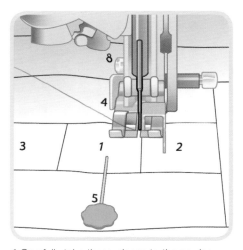

4 Carefully take these pieces to the sewing machine and sew on the line between segments one and two. You always sew from the side of the printed lines, and fabric is always placed on the blank side of the pattern.

**Tip**
Sewing on to paper will blunt your sewing machine needle, so keep a separate needle that you use just for FPP.

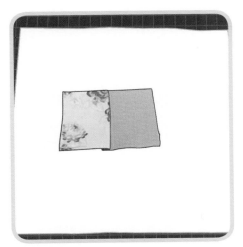

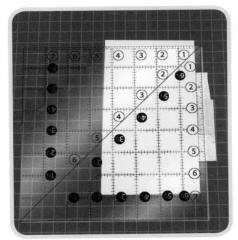

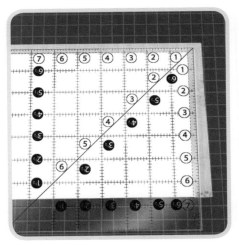

**5** Finger press the piece over the second segment from the right side.

**6** Fold the paper template in half on the line you just sewed and flip the second piece back on itself so that the seam allowance of the pieces is the only thing sticking out from the edge of the paper. Trim this to ¼ inch using your ruler.

**7** Continue pinning, stitching, flipping and trimming until all the segments are covered.

**8** Square up the block from the reverse side, trimming the seam allowance around the edge as per instructions on paper template. Tear off the paper, being careful not to pop any of the stitches.

## Tip

Set your sewing machine to a short stitch length (1–1.5) so that your stitches don't pop when you tear the paper off later.

## Binding a Quilt

The standard method of finishing a quilt is to use straight grain double fold binding. It gives the project a clean finished look and is a strong edge finish. If your project has curved corners, you will need to use bias binding. Bias binding is cut on the bias of the fabric, i.e. at a 45-degree angle to the selvedge. This makes it liable to stretch and distort, which is exactly what you need when binding circular objects.

1 Measure the circumference of your quilt and add 10 inches. Divide this figure by 42 (the width of your fabric) and round up to the nearest whole number. Cut this many binding strips from fabric. If using straight grain binding, cut these strips from selvedge to selvedge.

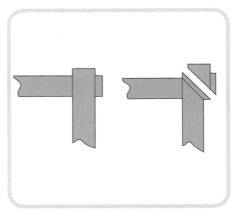

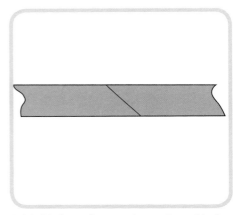

2 If using bias binding, cut at a 45-degree angle to the selvedge. I like to use 2½-inch width strips for double fold binding to give a slightly thicker and more defined edge, although some quilters prefer 2¼ inches. Decide what works for you.

3 Join binding strips to make one long strip. I join the short edges and sew straight across with ¼-inch seam, but you can also join with a 45-degree angle to separate the bulk of the seam. To do this, lay your pieces RST and perpendicular to each other. Sew a diagonal line starting and ending at the intersection of the pieces. Trim excess fabric ¼ inch from the seam and press open.

4 Iron the long strip in half lengthways. On one of the short ends, press under ½ inch to the wrong side.

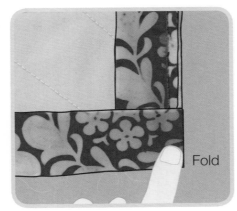

Fold

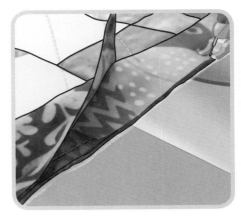

**5** Starting with the pressed-under end, align the binding strip with the raw edge of the quilt. Make sure to start in the middle of one of the quilt edges. Open up the folded binding and sew the first 5 inches through just one layer with a ¼-inch seam allowance. This secures the beginning of the binding, but leaves the pocket open to slot the tail-end in later.

**6** Fold binding back in half properly, and begin stitching approximately 6 inches from the start of the strip. Sew the whole length of the side, stopping and backstitching when you reach ¼ inch from the end.

**7** Fold strip back on itself to make a 45-degree angle in the corner, and the tail-end of the strip continues the line of the next edge to be sewn.

**8** Fold strip back on itself again so that the resulting fold is aligned with the edge you just sewed, and the tail-end is now perfectly in line with the next edge to be sewn.

**9** Begin sewing right from the edge of the quilt. Repeat steps six–eight until the last corner is done.

**10** When you are within 5 inches of the starting point, trim the tail of the binding strip so it overlaps the starting point by approximately 2 inches. Slot the tail inside the pocket you made in step five, and continue sewing along the edge. Make sure to continue just past the starting stitches and backstitch to secure.

## Finishing the Binding

There are now two ways to finish the binding, by hand or by machine. Hand stitching, although a much longer process, has the benefits of being nearly invisible, very precise and very neat. Machine stitching is much quicker, may be stronger, but is not as easy to get a nice finish. I suggest trying both ways to see which works for you.

### By Hand

**1** Thread a length of cotton thread approximately 18 inches and tie a knot in one end. If possible, match the thread colour to the binding, not the backing.

**2** Fold the binding from the front to the back so that the fold just covers the seam line. Pin or clip in place along the length. I love Wonder Clips by Clover for this job.

**3** Use a blind stitch to stitch the binding to the back of the quilt, taking care that the stitches go through the backing and batting but not the front.

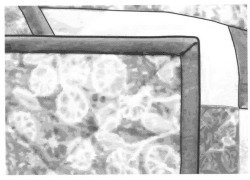

Front

**4** When you reach a corner, the mitre should fall into place fairly easily.

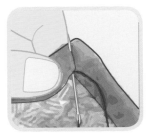

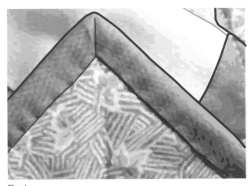

Back

**5** Take two or three stitches into the corner to secure and continue around the quilt.

## By Machine

1 Fold binding from the front to the back so that the edge of the fold just covers the seam line. Pin in place along the circumference of the quilt.

2 Using the sewing machine, stitch so that you catch the edge of the binding and are sewing slightly to the left of the first seam line. If you move to the right, the stitching line will appear on the binding at the front. If you move too far to the left, the stitching line will go into the quilt.

3 Keep sewing around the quilt until you finish where you started. Try to be accurate when you are sewing; it is difficult to keep the stitching just to the left of the seam line, so check regularly. This is how it should look.

## Useful Hand Stitches

### Quilters' Knot

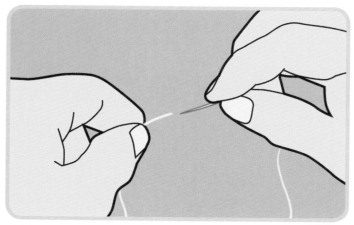

1 Hold the threaded needle in your right hand thumb and forefinger, and the tail-end of the thread in your left so that the tips are facing.

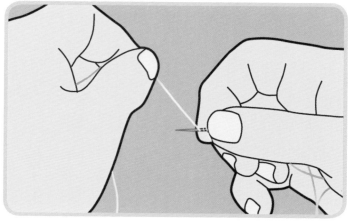

2 Transfer the tail-end to your right hand and wrap the loop of thread around the needle with your left three–six times depending on thickness.

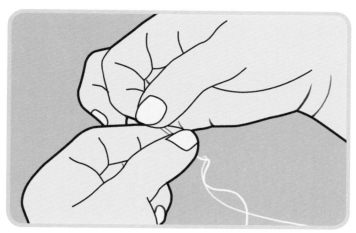

3 Hold the wraps and thread tail with left hand thumb and forefinger, then use your free right hand to pull the needle up.

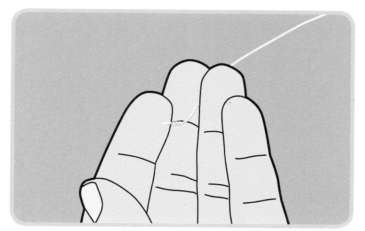

4 Slide the wraps all the way down the length of thread and pull tight to form a small knot.

## Blind Stitch

Often used for quilt binding:

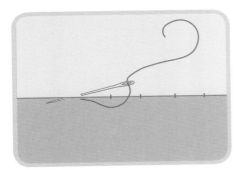

**1** Hide knot in seam allowance, come up through the folded edge.

**2** Make a small vertical stitch to secure the folded edge to the backing.

**3** Travel approximately ½ inch through the batting, coming up through the folded edge. Repeat.

## Whip Stitch

Often used for joining EPP:

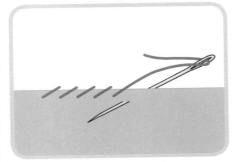

**1** Hold two fabric pieces together and make a stitch through both pieces from back to front, close to the edge.

**2** Bring needle and thread up and over the pieces.

**3** Make a second stitch, again from back to front. Stitches are always made the same way.

## Ladder Stitch

Often used for invisible-close turning holes:

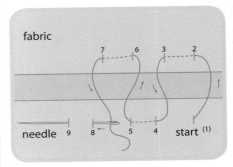

**1** Follow the numbered points in the above image to create a ladder stitch.

**2** After every 2 inches, pull the thread taut to close and hide the stitches.

## Appliqué

Appliqué is the age-old method of securing a shape to a background piece of fabric. It is often used where more complex designs are desired and negates the need for piecing complicated shapes. The basic process involves cutting one shape out of one piece of fabric, using a method (discussed below) to fuse it to the background, and stitching around the edge to secure. The edge stitching can be decorative, such as a thick outlined blanket stitch, or invisible, as in needle-turned appliqué.

## Raw Edge Appliqué

There are numerous brands of fusible web, namely Bondaweb, Steam-a-Seam, Heat-n-Bond and Wonder Under, which can be used with raw edge appliqué. The process for all is very similar, but do follow the individual manufacturers instructions.

**1** Draw a shape on the paper side of the fusible web. Roughly cut out leaving a large seam allowance.

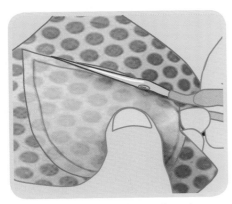

**2** Adhere fusible side of drawn shape to wrong side of fabric and cut out exactly on the drawn line. Peel off the paper layer to reveal the fusible side. Position on to the background fabric and secure in place permanently by pressing with a hot iron.

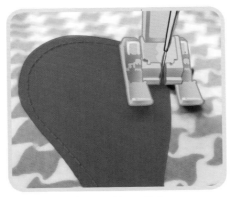

**3** Using a sewing machine, stitch on, or very close to, the edge of the shape. A straight stitch can be used, and the shape can be outlined multiple times to create a sketch effect. Alternatively, use a blanket, zigzag or other decorative stitch and only outline once.

## Hand Appliqué

The process of hand appliqué undoubtedly takes longer than raw edge, but it can give a much more refined look to the quilt. Many traditional quilts were made this way, taking years to complete an intricate design.

## Using Templates

**1** Make paper, card or freezer paper template of finished size of shape.

**2** Draw around template (or if using freezer paper, fuse the shape) on to the wrong side of the fabric and cut out neatly with ¼ inch seam allowance. Clip into any points for ease of pressing.

**3** Turn the seam allowance under to the wrong side by pressing with an iron. Use spray starch to stabilise more difficult shapes.

**4** If using freezer paper, remove it and pin or glue-baste the shape to the background and secure with a ladder or slip stitch.

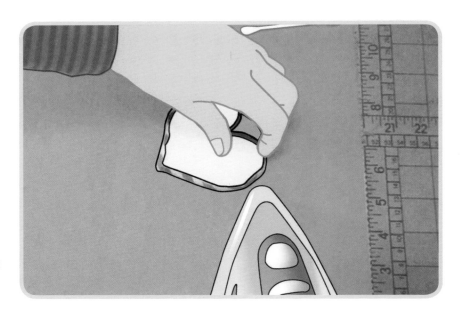

## Using Needle Turn

**1** Use a template to draw shape directly on to RS of fabric with a washable marker. Cut out neatly with ¼ inch seam allowance.

**2** Pin shape to background fabric using appliqué pins.

**3** Turn under the seam allowance with the point of the needle as you work your way around the shape, slip stitching as you go.

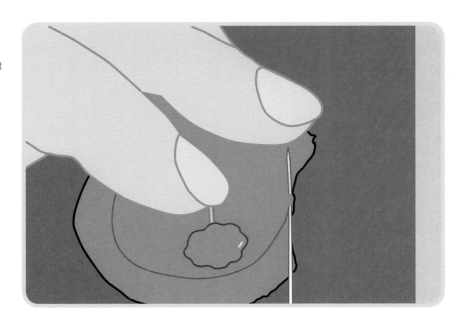

## Reverse Appliqué

Reverse appliqué creates little windows in the background fabric so focal fabrics can shine through. It works particularly well with knitted fabric for the background as this will not fray.

**1** Using a washable fabric marker, draw design on to WS of focal fabric.

**2** Layer background fabric, WS facing, with focal fabric on top, WS facing. Pin to secure.

**3** Using a short stitch length (1.5) on your sewing machine, stitch around the drawn line.

**4** Trim away the excess focal fabric, ¼ inch outside the sewn line.

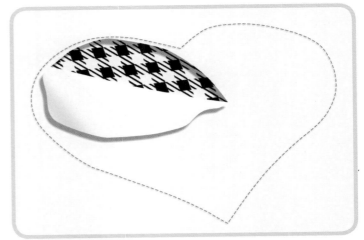

**5** Flip over and trim the background fabric from inside the sewn shape, cutting as close to the sewn line as possible.

## The Quilt Sandwich

The main method used by quilters to construct their quilts is what's known as a quilt sandwich. This is a three-layer process whereby the quilt backing and the quilt top are placed wrong sides together (the bread), with a layer of batting in the middle (the filling). The layers are then temporarily fixed together to stop any shifting or moving during quilting, using a process known as basting.

Basting a quilt involves temporarily securing the three layers of fabric together. This can be done with spray adhesive, basting pins or tacking stitches. With the pin and stitched basting methods, the set-up process is the same. Which process you use is entirely personal choice. Spray basting is quick and works particularly well on smaller projects. Pin basting or hand basting takes a little more time, but works better on larger quilts. Pins and basting stitches have to be removed, however, during the quilting process.

### Set-Up Process

1 Begin by smoothing out the back of the quilt, wrong side facing, on a hard surface. Using masking tape or painters' tape, secure the edges of the fabric. Do not tape the corners as this can cause the bias to distort.

2 Lay the batting on top, again smoothing any wrinkles as you go.

3 Finally, lay the quilt top – right side facing – on top of the batting. Use your hands to smooth out the wrinkles, working from the centre outwards. When you are happy with the sandwich, you can begin basting.

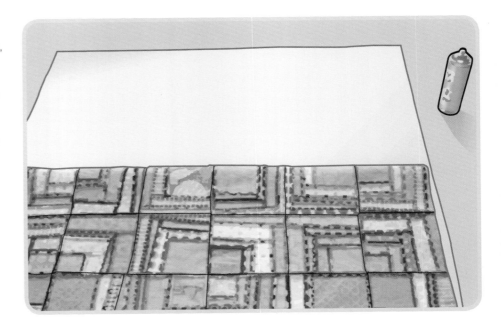

## Pin Basting

If using safety pins, work from the centre outwards, aiming to add a pin every 4–6 inches. While normal safety pins will strictly work, there are pins designed specially for this purpose. They have a curved design so they are much easier to hook through the layers. There is also a tool available called the Kwik Klip which makes opening and latching the safety pins much easier on the hands; a knitting needle will also work in a pinch.

## Hand Basting

If using tacking stitches, take a long length of contrasting coloured thread and a sharp needle. Start by hand sewing a line of large running stitches across the centre point both widthways and lengthways. Aim for each stitch to be about 1–1½ inches in size. Secure your stitches with a knot at the beginning. Aim to leave a tail of 1–2 inches so that the thread lines don't pull loose. Continue in this manner, creating a grid across the quilt until you have lines spaced every 6 inches.

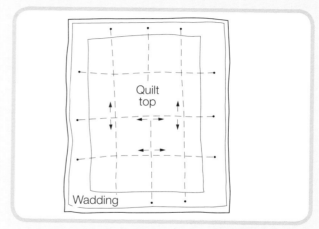

Quilt top

Wadding

## Tip

For pin basting, I like to work on a carpeted floor; it grips the fabric slightly on the back to help with smoothing out wrinkles and offers some slight cushioning for the knees. When spray basting, I like to work outside or on my kitchen floor for easy cleanup. If you don't have a floor space big enough to accommodate the size of quilt you are basting, it is possible to baste in two halves on a dining table. Just smooth as best you can and roll up one half. Pin or spray and unroll as you go.

## Spray Basting

If using spray adhesive, there is no need to secure the backing fabric to the surface. Begin by protecting your work surface with an old sheet or plastic layer. Be sure to work in a well ventilated area. Some quilters prefer to do this process outside.

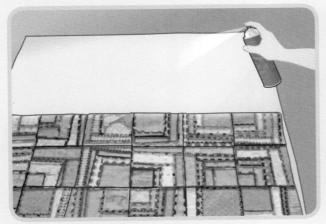

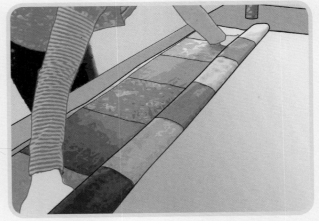

**1** Lay the batting on the surface, and smooth the quilt top on to it, right side facing. When wrinkle free, peel and fold back one half of the top, widthwise.

**2** Apply spray adhesive to a section of the batting, approximately 12 inches wide and across the whole width of the quilt, just next to the folded section.

**3** Slide your hands under the folded edge and push the fold forward so that the quilt top rolls over the adhered section of batting. Use a swimming motion with your hands to smooth wrinkles forward and to the sides.

**4** Repeat the folding back, spraying and smoothing process until you reach the end of the quilt and repeat for the second half. Flip the sandwich over and repeat for the backing.

## Alternative Quilting Styles

### Quilt-As-You-Go

The quilt-as-you-go (QAYG) method is useful for larger projects (which might be a struggle to fit through a domestic machine), improvised style designs, and strip-based projects. There are two kinds of QAYG techniques: one when you have quilt blocks already made, and another when you build your quilt block as you go.

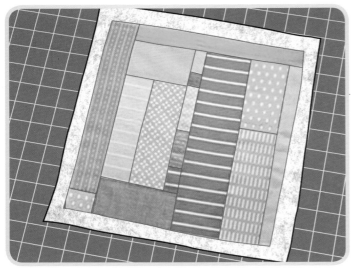

Begin by cutting a square of batting 1 inch larger than your block. Choose a natural fibre batting that can withstand heat from pressing with a steam iron.

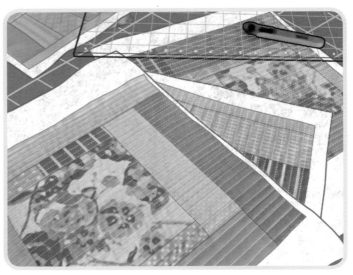

If you are using pre-made quilt blocks, baste your quilt block on to the batting and quilt as desired. Note, no backing fabric is used. Once quilted, trim and square to desired size.

## Stitch and Flip Technique

To build your quilt block up as you go, you will need to use the stitch and flip technique. This works particularly well with log cabin blocks and strip piecing.

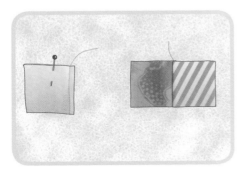

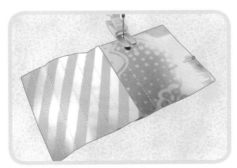

1 Using a log cabin as an example, lay your centre square, right side facing, in the centre of the batting. Place the first log, right sides together, with the square and stitch a ¼-inch seam. This not only sews the pieces together, but also affixes them to the batting.

2 Open the piece out, finger press, and quilt over the top of both pieces. Add the second log in the same manner, laying right sides together with the previous two pieces, stitching and flipping. I like to add between three and four quilting lines per log.

3 Continue until the block is the desired size.

4 Square block to desired size, either by using a large square ruler or by lining up with the marks on your cutting mat. It is vitally important that the block is square and the same size on each edge.

## For both methods, to join the QAYG blocks:

1 Arrange in the desired layout and piece into rows and columns using a ½-inch seam allowance.

2 Press seam allowance open using a hot steam iron, trimming at edges of block (as shown) to reduce bulk.

3 When the top is pieced, baste on to the backing fabric and stitch in the ditch through all the block joins. This will create a grid of quilting on the backing. You could choose to do more quilting at this stage i.e. diagonal lines through, or ties in the centre, of each block.

4 Bind as desired.

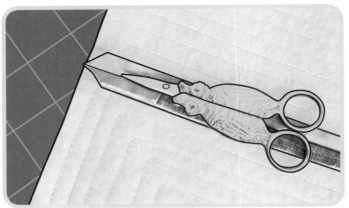

## Bagging Out

Bagging out, also known as a pillowcase finish, is the process of sewing the layers of a quilt wrong sides together, and turning through a small gap. It negates the need for binding and is an interesting alternative finish for smaller projects.

**1** Layer the pieces with backing and quilt top RS together, WS of quilt top facing, followed by batting.

**2** Pin all layers together securely and sew a ½-inch seam around the perimeter of the sandwich with the batting facing towards you. Make sure to backstitch at the beginning and end of your stitching line, and leave a 6-inch gap for turning (or smaller for a smaller item).

**3** Clip the corners and trim the batting to a scant ¼-inch all the way around the sandwich.

**4** Turn through to the right side, poke corners out with a turning tool, and press.

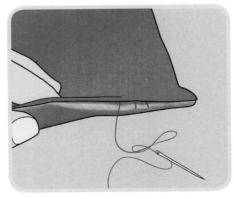

**5** Pin the turning gap closed and use a ladder stitch to secure. Top stitch all the way around the quilt, ¼ inch from the edge. You could add quilting at this stage, making sure you knot and bury your thread ends inside the quilt (optional).

## Tied Quilts

Tying a quilt is an alternative to machine or hand quilting. It is much faster, gives a softer look, and is suitable for thicker fabrics such as denim. Many different threads/yarns can be used for tying as long as they are strong and sturdy. You could try wool yarn, perle cotton, stranded embroidery thread, hand-quilting thread, or even thin ribbon. You will need a sharp needle with an eye large enough to hold your tying thread.

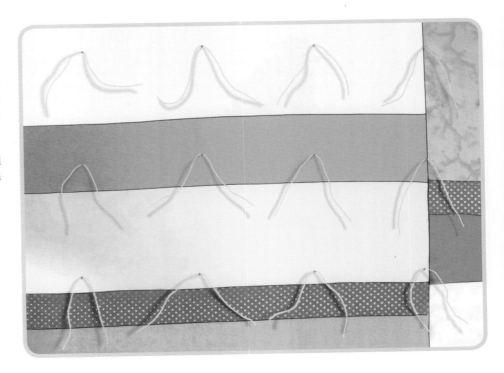

1 Begin by making the quilt sandwich: backing, batting and quilt top.

2 Using a ruler and an erasable fabric pen, mark a grid on the quilt top where you will place your ties, every 4–6 inches is advised. Pin-baste the sandwich, placing a pin in each of the marks. You will remove one row of pins at a time as you tie the quilt.

3 Thread a long length of yarn on to the needle. Make a ¼-inch stitch at the first mark, starting and ending at the front of the quilt. Leave a long tail of 6 inches as you pull the yarn through, and move on to the next mark. Do not cut the yarn in between stitches; leave it slack. When you have finished the row, cut the yarn leaving another long tail of approximately 6 inches. Repeat until all rows have been sewn.

4 Working one row at a time, snip the yarn at the mid point between each stitch. Tie the two loose ends of each stitch into a square or reef knot. This is a simple double knot; hold one thread tail in each hand and cross the right thread over the left thread. Pull it under the left thread to form a single knot. Repeat this motion once more, crossing the left thread over the right. Repeating the mantra 'Right over left and under, left over right and under' helps. When all the loose ends have been tied, trim the tails to a uniform length of 1–1½ inches.

# Further Skills

# Further Skills

It's the finishing touches, like quilting, labelling and displaying your quilt that give it that special handmade charm. One of my friends once said to me that binding a quilt by hand was her favourite because she took that time to get to know the quilt. That thought stuck with me ever since; it's worth taking your time over these little details to truly personalise and learn to love your creation.

## Choosing Quilting Designs for the Project

When you have finished your quilt top, most patterns will direct you to 'quilt as desired'. This can be a baffling instruction to quilters of any ability. To choose a type of quilting for your project, think about its intended use. Does it need to be particularly hard wearing? Is the quilting the main focus of the project? Are you going for a geometric look or a softer look?

A few key points to remember:
- The denser the quilting, the less drape the quilt has.
- Quilting should look balanced; there shouldn't be vast areas un-quilted, nor should the quilting be too bunched up.
- Match thread colour to background or sashing.
- Use the same colour top and bottom thread to avoid highlighting tension issues.

Regardless of the quilting style, if your machine has a 'needle down' position, engage it. This means every time you stop sewing, the needle stays in the quilt. It will ensure any straight lines don't go wobbly, and any free motion quilting stitch lengths don't get longer.

**All-over quilting** is where a single design is replicated across the whole quilt. This can include free motion or straight line designs.

**Bespoke quilting** is where individual blocks or block sections are quilted in different ways to enhance the shapes and patterns. Many quilters send their completed quilt tops to a Long Arm Quilter, who can provide intricate bespoke quilting as well as simpler computerised all-over or edge-to-edge designs.

## Fabric Markers

There are many options available to mark a design on to a basted quilt top. Some quilters mark out the whole design, and others use a more freehand technique. If using any of the fabric markers below, be sure to test on a small piece of your fabric first.

**Air Vanishing** Generally purple in ink colour, these felt tip markers will disappear over time. Note: I have experienced these marks returning after some time, so would not recommend them for use on white fabric.

**Water Soluble** Generally blue in ink colour, these felt tip markers disappear when sprayed with water.

**Frixion Markers** Available in many standard ink colours, these roller-ball pens will disappear when ironed or rubbed with the special base on the end of the pen. They can be found online as well as in stationery stores.

**Hera Marker** This is a little plastic tool that is used to score lines in the quilt top. If you can't find one locally, you can use a palette knife in a pinch.

You don't have to mark every line you intend to sew on the quilt top. If, for example, you are quilting lines 1 inch apart, you may wish to mark every 5 inches and use the quilting bar guide on your machine set to a 1-inch gap to fill in between.

## Hand Quilting

Hand quilting is a traditional way of securing the three layers of the quilt together permanently. The stitches are visible on both sides of the quilt and add a lovely soft homemade feel. There are many different ways to achieve the hand-quilted look. It is a lengthy process, so you should find the way that works best for you and be comfortable in your stitching.

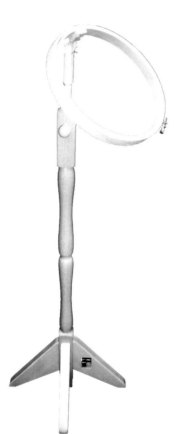

Quilting hoops and frames are very similar to embroidery hoops, but they have a thinner and wider ring.

Some are round, some are square, and some have stands for the floor or for your lap. They all serve the same purpose however, to keep the quilt layers taut while you are sewing. They are not mandatory for hand quilting; I do not use a hoop or frame when hand quilting as I prefer to just hold the quilt in my hands.

Specialist hand quilting threads are available that are not suitable for use on the sewing machine. They have a 'glazed' coating to prevent knotting and tangling.

I like a nice thick stitch for hand quilting; if I've painstakingly placed every stitch, I want to be able to see them. My thread of choice would be Perle cotton #8.

Perle cotton is a 2-ply thread which has a similar thickness to stranded embroidery thread but cannot be separated. You can also use embroidery thread for hand quilting, but it is not as strong as the specialist threads.

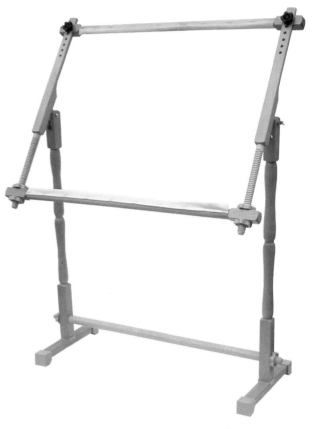

A selection of needlework stretcher bars and hoops can be used for embroidery, canvas work and quilting. The advantage of a large stand is that both hands are left free to work. The fabric must be laced into position, whereas on stretcher bars without a stand, pins or drawing pins can be used.

Smaller circular hoops are only used for fine needlework. They are made from two loops that can be tightened by a screw, between which the fabric is trapped. Whenever hoops or stretcher bars are being used, make sure the fabric is evenly stretched with no wrinkles or buckling.

## How to Hand Quilt

Decide what kind of pattern you would like, and mark it on the basted quilt top. This could range from straight lines to outline quilting, or a complex whole-cloth style design. I would suggest that beginners try outline stitching. If you have pressed your seams to the side when piecing the block, then you can follow the seam line underneath. Your stitches will be straight and there will be no need to mark.

1 Take a length of thread as long as your forearm and make a quilter's knot in one end (see directions on page 56). Thread on to the needle. Wear a thimble on the middle finger of the dominant hand. Take needle down into the quilt, through the top and batting (but not backing) 1 inch from where you want to start your first stitch. Travel along through the centre of the quilt, coming up where you want to start the stitch.

2 Pull the thread taut so the knotted end sits just on the quilt top. Then give a short sharp tug to pop the knot through the fabric.

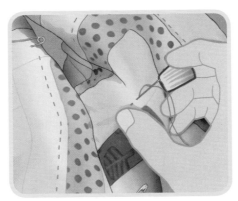

3 Take your first stitch by entering the quilt with your needle point at a vertical angle. Your dominant hand will push from the top using the thimbled middle finger. Your other hand will feel from the bottom when the needle comes through. Once the point is through the backing, you simultaneously rock the needle with your middle finger and push forward slightly and consistently to make your stitch length.

4 Repeat this rocking motion until you have picked up four to five stitches.

5 Pull thread through all stitches, being careful not to create too much puckering.

6 Repeat steps three–five until you reach the end of your stitching line. Make your final stitch, and then bring the needle through the centre of the quilt and up again close to the stitch.

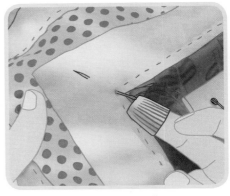

7 Tie a knot that lays on the quilt top.

8 Take your needle down into the quilt again, come up 1 inch away, and pull the knot through. Snip thread tails to finish.

Christmas Bauble Baby
Quilt, page 146.

## Machine Quilting

All domestic sewing machines can be used for quilting. When quilting
a large quilt, the 'throat size' of the machine, i.e. the space between the
needle and the body of the machine, is important; the larger the better.
However, that is not to say great results cannot be achieved on even the
most basic domestic machines. An extension table can also be applied to
the sewing machine to increase the working area.

## Straight Line Quilting

For straight line quilting, it is advisable to use a walking/even-feed
foot. This enables both the top and bottom layers of the quilt to be
pulled through the machine at an even speed. It prevents bunching
and ruffling on the top of the quilt and often gives a more regulated
stitch length. Some machines have an integrated walking foot; for
others it is an optional attachment. Refer to your manual to check.

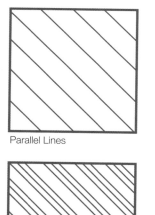

Parallel Lines

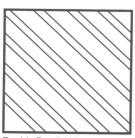

Double Parallel Lines

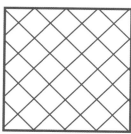

Diagonal Grid

Triple Parallel Lines

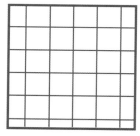

Vertical/Horizontal Lines

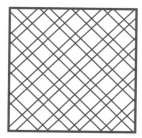

Check

1 Decide what kind of pattern you would
like and mark it on the basted quilt top:
diagonal, horizontal or vertical grid,
crosshatch, quarters, diamond, concentric
squares or concentric circles.

2 Starting with the centre line, sew all the
way along the line, starting and stopping on
the edge of the batting. If your design starts
and stops visibly on the quilt top, make sure
to draw up your bottom thread and leave
long tails so you can secure them in the
batting later.

3 Continue sewing each line across the quilt
top, working from the centre out.

## Free Motion Quilting

Free motion quilting (FMQ) is the process of 'drawing' a continuous line design on the quilt top, and you move the quilt (the paper), rather than the sewing machine (the pen). You will need a darning or open-toe foot for your machine to achieve this. You will also need to be able to drop the feed dogs so that you can move the quilt in all directions rather than just straight.

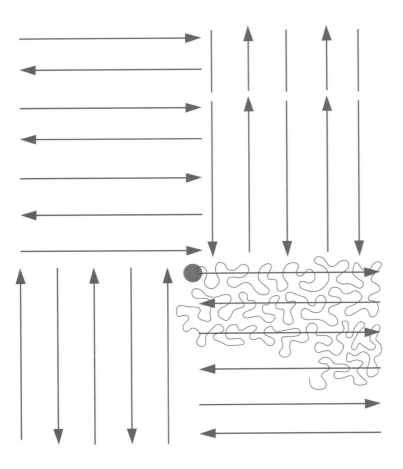

**1** Lower feed dogs and attach darning foot.

**2** Draw the bottom thread up through the quilt and pull long thread tails for securing later.

**3** Take two or three stitches in the same spot to secure, and then begin your quilting pattern.

**4** Continue quilting from the centre of the quilt outwards.

With an all-over design, you may find it easier to mentally mark the quilt into quadrants and work in one area at a time.

The kinds of designs you can create with FMQ are endless. Here are some examples:

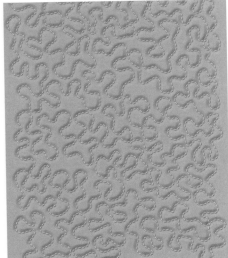

Stipple

Loops

Bubbles/Pebbles

Swirls

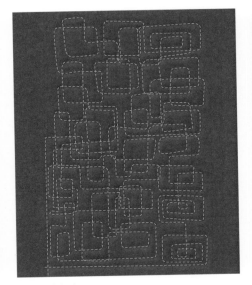

Square Stipple

Feathers

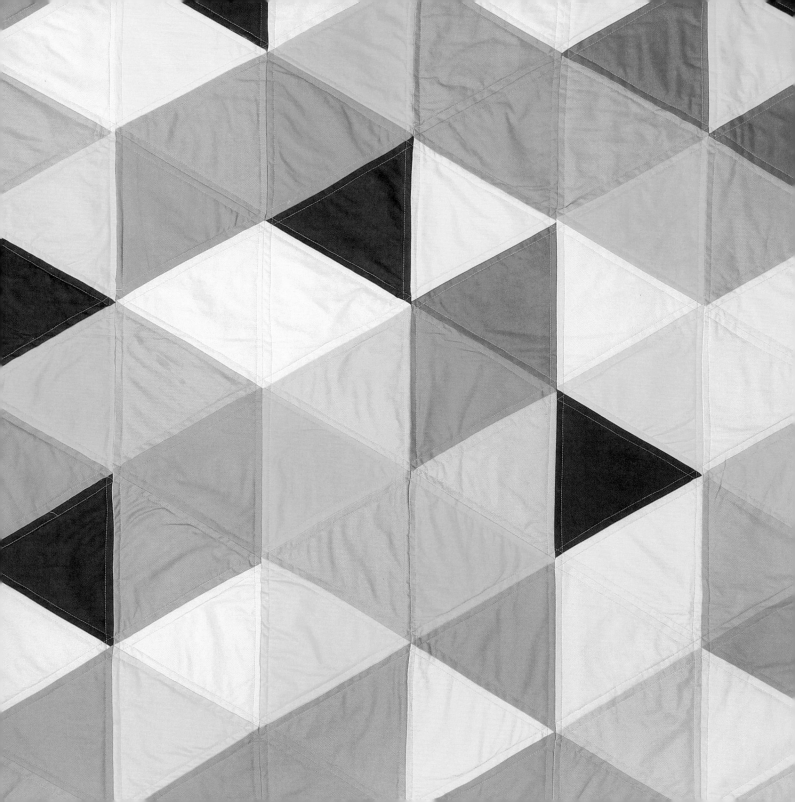

## Stitch in the Ditch

Stitching in the ditch is a method of quilting used to minimise the amount of stitched lines shown on the quilt top. The quilting line is sewn directly on the seam between blocks or borders. Because of this, the line tends to disappear when viewed from afar. The best results can be achieved when seams have been pressed to one side rather than open.

**1** Engage walking foot.

**2** Beginning with a central line, sew slowly and evenly along the seam. Take care not to wobble either side of the ditch.

**3** Working from the centre out, and starting and stopping on the batting where possible, repeat for the rest of the seam lines on the quilt top.

## Outline Quilting

Outline quilting is a very similar process, but is sewn either ⅛ inch or ¼ inch from the ditch. It is more popular with hand quilters because it avoids the bulk of the seam.

## Echo Quilting

To emphasise a patch or block pattern, echo quilting can be used. Begin by outline quilting once around the shape and coming back to finish exactly where you started. Secure threads. Then, outline quilt another line around the previous quilted line. Continue in this manner until the entire shape is filled. The width between stitching lines can be varied depending on the density of the quilting required.

Sherbet and Liquorice
Quilt, page 104.

## Labelling

Labelling your quilt is the last step of personalisation; it serves a practical purpose as well as decorative. If you are gifting or selling this quilt, you will want the recipient to know who made it and for what purpose. If your quilt is to be in a show, you will want to make sure your contact details are on the label in case it gets lost or anyone has an enquiry about it. If the quilt is for a new baby, you may wish to mark the date of their birth on the back as a keepsake for the parents.

### Hand-Written

A hand-written note on the back of a quilt adds so much sentiment. Can you imagine 100 years down the line when this is now a vintage quilt and someone finds it? The addition of your little message will bring them so much joy.

**1** Cut a piece of freezer paper the finished size of your label. Cut a piece of white fabric 1 inch larger than the freezer paper template all the way round.

**2** On the paper side of the freezer paper, draw lines spaced ½ inch.

**3** Iron the waxy side to the wrong side of your fabric, and write your message on to the fabric.

**4** Press the edges under, remove freezer paper, and appliqué to the quilt.

### Embroidered

If you are skilled at embroidery, hand stitched labels are something a little special. It is also a great idea for children's messages. Have your child write their name or draw around their hand on a piece of paper for you to trace on to the fabric and embroider.

**1** Cut a piece of fabric large enough to fit in an embroidery hoop.

**2** Use a washable fabric marker to write the design on to the fabric.

**3** Embroider over the top of the writing.

**4** Trim to 1 inch larger than desired size, press edges under and appliqué to quilt.

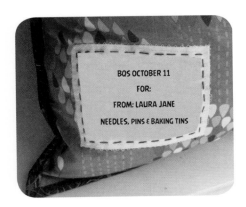

## Printed or Stamped

Specialist ink cartridges are available for most domestic printers which enable you to print on fabric. If you don't want to go to that expense however, I have had success with freezer paper-backed fabric and normal ink on my ink jet printer.

1 Take a piece of normal paper from your printer. Measure it and cut three pieces of freezer paper the same size.

2 Iron all three pieces of freezer paper to the back of your fabric – this gives it stability going through the printer.

3 Design your quilt label on your computer, load up the paper and click print.

4 Trim to 1 inch larger than desired size, press well to set the printer ink, press edges under and appliqué to quilt.

Alternatively, you can use a letter set of stamps and fabric ink (I use Versacraft) to stamp directly on to the fabric. This gives a kind of messy homemade look, which I like.

## Manufactured

This is my favourite method of creating quilt labels. I designed my own label template and used Spoonflower, a website where you can design and print your own fabric, to get them printed. It is a slightly more expensive way of doing it, but the interface is so easy to use that once you have your label template, you just upload it to the website and just choose how much fabric you want to buy. The fabric is then posted to you in one piece and you cut up the labels yourself.

My label is quite large, and as such I usually piece it into the backing of the quilt. This also means it's never going to fall off or be removed from the quilt.

## Displaying

How and where you choose to display your quilts is an entirely
personal choice. I like to have as many quilts out and in use as
possible; use it or lose it, I say. Quilts don't just have to live on beds
however, you can use them as wall decorations, sling them over the
sofa, lay them on a table or bench, even use them as floor mats. The
list is endless.

## Hanging Sleeve

If you want to hang your quilts on a wall or submit them for a
show you will need to make a hanging sleeve.

1 Cut a piece of fabric 9 inches tall x width of quilt. You may need to
piece this if your quilt is large.

2 Press short edges to the wrong side by turning under ¼ inch.
Repeat. Top stitch ⅛ inch from the edge.

3 Fold the strip in half lengthways WST, aligning raw edges.
Sew together with a ½-inch seam allowance. Press seam
allowance open.

4 Place the seam against the quilt back so that the top edge is
approximately ½ inch below the binding. Pin to quilt back.

5 Sew the top edge of the tube to the quilt backing using a whip
stitch. Make sure to catch both backing and batting layers without
coming through to the front.

6 Smooth the sleeve downward along the quilt back, and then pull up
by ½ inch along the length to create extra space. Pin in place.

7 Sew the bottom edge of the tube to the quilt using a whip stitch.

8 Sew the back side edges of the sleeve to the quilt. Do not sew the
front side edges down – this is where the rod or rail is inserted.

## Using Charm Squares

Another option for smaller quilts is to use folded charm squares in the
corners. A wooden dowel is slotted into each corner and can be hung
on wall hooks. This is not suitable for larger quilts because the weight
of the quilt would pull it out of shape.

1 Before binding your quilt, take 2 x 5-inch charm squares and press in
half to form triangles. Top stitch along the fold, ¼ inch from the edge.

2 Align raw edges of triangles and quilt in the top left and top right
corners and stitch down using ¼-inch seam allowance.

3 Attach binding as usual to the front of the quilt.

4 When stitching the binding down on the back, make sure to go
through the pocket layers as well as the batting and backing.

Can be machine washed

Hand wash only

Do not iron

## Laundering

It is a fact that quilts will get old and worn over time. I'm okay with that because it means they've been used. Why make a quilt if not to use it? They are, after all, functional items. But there are several steps you can take to ensure the longevity of your quilt.

If your quilt is made with 100 per cent cotton fabrics, there is no reason why it cannot be laundered on a cool wash cycle and loaded into the dryer. I like to tumble my quilts to give them that smooshy antique feel. There is nothing quite like a quilt fresh from the dryer.

## Colour Fastness

This is a hugely important test before you wash your quilt. Having made the mistake of not testing once before and ruining a beautiful white quilt, I now test everything I am unsure about. The most common colours that would run in the washing machine are red, dark pink, black, dark blue and dark purple. Basically, any dark colours where the fabric may have retained some of the dye. In my experience, most quilting weight cotton by well-known manufacturers is fine, but basics, backings and extra wides are worth testing.

To test for colour fastness, cut a 5-inch square of test fabric and a 5-inch square of white fabric. Leave in a bowl of warm soapy water for 20 minutes, agitating the fabric and stirring periodically. If there is any dye transfer to the white fabric when both pieces are dry, then I would advise you pre-wash the fabric.

Pre-washing is a great way to avoid the situation above. This simply involves putting any new fabric through the washer and dryer before using it. Some quilters are in favour of this, and some don't bother. I am in the don't bother camp and would just pre-wash if and when I thought it was needed.

**Tip**
The first couple of times I wash a quilt I use at least three 'colour catchers' in the drum. This makes sure any accidental bleeding gets sucked up by the catchers and not by the quilt.

## Storing Your Quilts

The best place to store quilts is flat on a bed, away from direct sunlight. However, if you do need to store in a cupboard, be wary of folding the quilt too tightly. Cotton fabric retains folds quite well, which means if your quilt is constantly folded the same way, it may begin to develop permanent fold lines.

If space is at a premium, quilts can be rolled together for storage. Always begin rolling from the top edge of the quilt so that when it is unrolled and hung, gravity will help to pull out the creases.

For long-term storage, it is advisable to store quilts in a 100 per cent cotton bag. This will protect from spills and dust, and will be chemical free. Do not store quilts in plastic bags; these may perish over time and cause the fabric to become compromised.

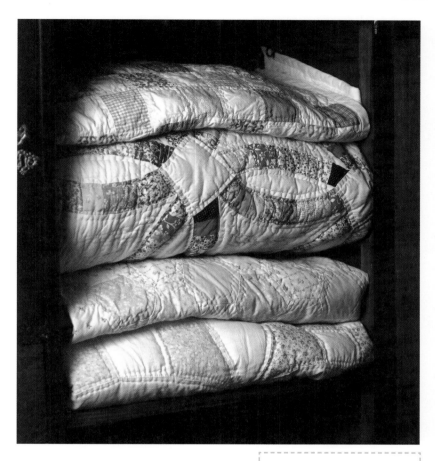

**Tip**

Polyester-based batting is great for not creasing. If you are doing a lot of trunk shows and need your quilts to look pristine after being folded for some time, a poly batting might be a good choice for you.

# Projects

# Project Selector

Whether you're looking for something simple, intermediate or advanced, use these pages to choose the quilt project you want to make.

## Simple Projects

These simple projects are the perfect way to get to grips with the basics. With a varied selection of designs to choose from, there is something for everyone.

**104 Sherbet and Liquorice Quilt**

**109 Rainbow Road Quilt**

**110 Painter's Palette Pillow**

**112 Starry Eyed Pillow**

## Intermediate Projects

These intermediate projects give you the next step up in quilting skills. Try these projects to build confidence and expertise before moving on to the advanced quilts.

**124 Seaglass Quilt**

**128 Baby Steps Quilt**

**133 Liberty Style Wall Hanging**

**134 Happy Picnic Table Runner**

## Advanced Projects

These advanced projects test your ability and let you create a great selection of impressive items. Use these projects to make something really special.

**156 Picnic Posy Quilt**

**158 Churn Dashing**

**161 Sew and Go Tote**

**164 Postcards from Japan Wall Hanging**

Sew and Go Tote, page 161

Snack Sack, page 141

**115 Feathered Friends Pillow**

**116 Laptop Sleeve**

**119 Pincushions**

**137 Potholders**

**141 Snack Sack**

**142 Pinwheel Pouch**

**147 Christmas Bauble Baby Quilt**

**148 Obsession Quilt**

**153 His 'n' Hers Stockings**

**167 Welcome Home Pillow**

**170 Honeycomb Table Centre**

**173 Cityscape Table Mats**

**175 Laptop Case**

**178 Travel Sewing Kit**

**182 Rock Around a Snowball Table Runner**

# Sherbet and Liquorice Quilt

Equilateral triangles bring a modern and geometric feel to any quilt, and using only solid fabrics for the quilt top makes it even more striking. The triangles make the quilt really interesting to look at as your brain tries to rationalise the shapes you are seeing. Being fairly addicted to prints, going for a completely solid look is a challenge for me and is why I have used so many colours. This quilt would look equally striking in a mix of solids and prints, or all prints.

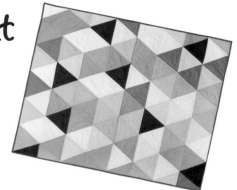

## Materials

- Strips: 12 x (8 inches x WOF); Robert Kaufman Kona Cottons in
  Charcoal,
  Pomegranate,
  Papaya,
  Banana,
  Sage,
  Pear,
  Lavender,
  Carnation,
  Blue,
  Ice Frappe,
  Violet,
  Peapod
- Backing: 2½ yds flannel; Timeless Treasures Sketch Flannel in Charcoal
- Binding: 6 x (2½-inch x WOF) strips; Robert Kaufman Kona Cotton in Glacier

## Finished Measurements

- 46 x 58 inches

## Instructions

1 From each 8-inch WOF strip, sub-cut eight equilateral triangles using the instructions in the techniques section (page 43).

2 Join all 96 triangles into pairs by placing RST and sewing down one edge.

3 Join pairs into sets of four by placing two pairs at an angle, offsetting the points by ¼ inch each side, and sewing down the edge.

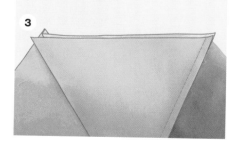

4 Arrange the sets of four into eight rows of three sets. Join sets to make the quilt top.

5 Trim top square by lining up the ¼-inch mark on your ruler with the points in the 'valley' of the triangles.

6 Baste, quilt and bind as desired. I chose to quilt in straight lines to complement the geometric look of the quilt. I stitched a line approximately ¼ inch from every seam line. This creates a funky star pattern on the front and back where the seams converge.

## Tip

Many quilters struggle with achieving a totally random look to their quilts. The key is to not over-think the placement of colours. To achieve the random layout with this quilt I used the very technical method of jumbling all the pieces up on the table, grabbing two that were closest with the only criteria being that they were different colours, and sewing them together. When there are only a small number of pieces left, it is advisable to pair them up before sewing, so that you are not left with too many of the same colour. I repeated this method for the whole quilt, and then pieced the rows. You will see there are some of the same colours touching, but I think this only adds to the random effect.

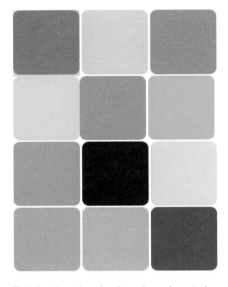

To help when choosing the colours, I created a
colour diagram of potential solids.

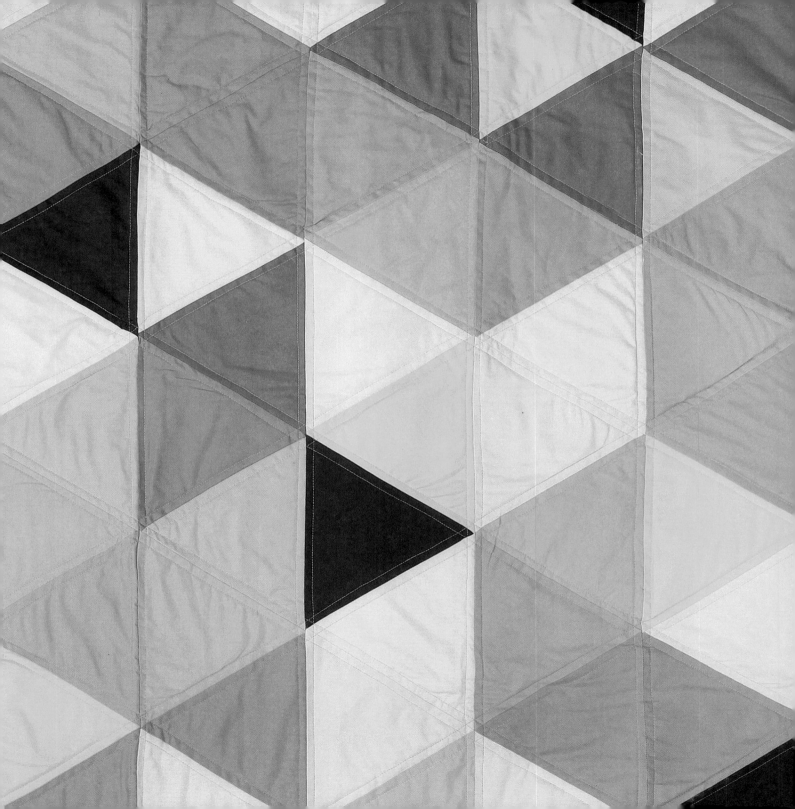

### Tip

One of my favourite ways to choose fabrics for a quilt is by colour matching. For this quilt, I started with a bundle of Pearl Bracelet Fat 8ths and picked a co-ordinating print for each one. It gives the quilt much more depth than just using one fabric. Another great way to do this is by matching a solid to a print. If you are stuck finding a perfect match, look for prints by the same designer or by a different designer under the same manufacturer.

# Rainbow Road Quilt

Great for adults and children alike, fun and funky fabrics breathe a new lease of life into a traditional single wedding ring quilt block. Try fussy cutting precious fabrics for the centre or using two different fabrics for the rectangle and square parts of the ring.

## Materials

- Rings: 12 x Fat 8ths;
  Andover Fabrics – Lizzy House –
  Pearl Bracelets in
  Frosting,
  Grape Jelly,
  Cosmonaut,
  Anchor,
  Ice Skate,
  Juniper,
  Swiss Chard,
  Basil,
  Verbena,
  Meyer Lemon,
  Persimmon,
  Watermelon
- Centres: 12 x (4½-inch) sqs
- BKG: 1 yd; Timeless Treasures
  in Sketch (Black on White)
- Batting: 40 x 50 inches
- Backing: 1½ yds;
  Ikea Alphabet duvet set
- Binding: ½ yd

## Finished Measurements

- 36 x 48 inches

## Instructions

1 Make 12 single wedding ring blocks according to the block directory on page 208.

2 Join the 12 blocks into four rows of three, then join the rows together to make the quilt top, following the layout below.

3 Baste, quilt and bind as desired. I quilted this with free motion circles, known as pebble or bubble quilting.

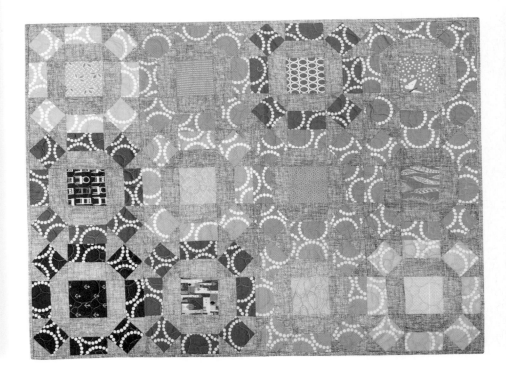

# Painter's Palette Pillow

This pillow uses a technique known as 'ticker tape' to create a quick and fun design piece. Choose your favourite colour palette and work with your fabric scraps for an inexpensive and fun project.

## Materials

- BKG: 18 inches sq; Art Gallery Fabrics; Color Me Retro, Dulcette Lobelia
- Scrap sqs: 3 x (3 inches) from each of 16 colours
- Batting: 20 x 20 inches
- Lining: 20 x 20 inches
- Pillow backing: 18 inches sq; Spotlight Australia; Newsprint
- Zipper: 22 inches
- Pinking shears
- Spray baste
- Pillow: 18 inches sq

## Finished Measurements

- Approximately 17½ inches square

## Instructions

1 Using pinking shears, trim all 3-inch sqs an equal amount to give zigzag edges.

2 Press BKG fabric into quarters, twice, to create a grid of 16 squares.

3 Layer lining RS down, batting and BKG fabric RS facing, and baste using spray adhesive.

4 Centre and pin the 3-inch sqs into each segment of the BKG fabric in the desired order. Using co-ordinated thread, sew the sqs to the BKG fabric using a ¼-inch seam.

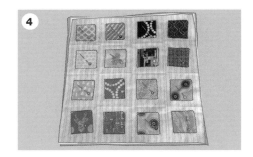

### Tip

Remember that ¼ inch of the pillow edges will become the seam allowance, so position your squares accordingly.

5 Quilt BKG of pillow as desired; I did a single line in between each sq. Trim excess batting and lining.

6 Using a pencil and ruler, mark ¼ inch either side of the zip teeth on reverse of the zip.

7 Place zip face down and centred on to the bottom edge of the pillow top, aligning pencil mark with edge of pillow. Sew using a zipper foot, as close to the teeth as possible. Press pillow top away from the zip, being careful not to melt the zip with the iron.

**8** Repeat step seven, placing zip (and attached pillow top) face down on to the bottom edge of the backing fabric. Align side seams of pillow top and backing fabric and sew using zipper foot.

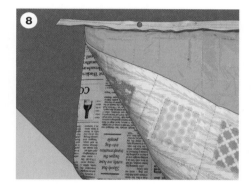

**9** Press backing fabric away from zip and top stitch both pieces ⅛ inch from the edge.

**10 IMPORTANT:** Open the zip slightly more than half way.

**11** Align side and bottom seams of pillow top and backing fabric and pin to secure.

**12** Sew around the three open sides of the pillow, backstitching at each end.

**13** Trim excess zip and overlock/serge/zigzag stitch the raw edges of the pillow. Turn RS out, poke out corners and stuff with an 18-inch pillow form.

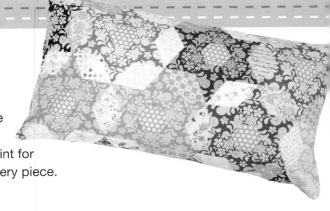

# Starry Eyed Pillow

The subtle tones of the low-volume background fabrics, coupled with the delicate but bright florals creates a pillow that is gentle on the eye and calming for the soul. I chose to use eight different colours of the same print for the stars but you could go really scrappy and use a different fabric for every piece.

## Materials

- Assorted fabric scraps
- Batting: 14 x 24 inches
- Backing: 2 x (10 x 22 inches)
- Wooden buttons: 4 x (¾ inches)
- Pillow insert: 12 x 21 inches
- Pillow: 12 x 21 inches

## Finished Measurements

- Approximately 12 x 21 inches

## Instructions

1 EPP the following shapes, including the templates on page 184:
8 Hexagons; 52 Jewels (six of six different colours, four of two different colours, one of eight different colours); 29 Diamonds.

2 Join the jewels and hexagons to make six full stars and two half stars.

3 Arrange with diamonds separating each star as in photograph. Join.

4 Place remaining jewels in spaces around the edge and piece together to make the rectangular pillow shape.

5 Press the pillow front, carefully remove papers, baste and quilt as desired. I chose wavy line quilting to maintain the softness of the project.

6 When quilted, line up the ¼-inch mark on your ruler with the tips of the star-points on one long side. Trim. Repeat on all sides, making sure the pillow is squared up.

7 For each of the backing rectangles, on one long side press ¼ inch towards the wrong side. On one piece, fold over again and press a further 2 inches, and on the other,

press 1½ inches. Top stitch each backing piece twice; once ⅛ inch from the edge to decorate and once ⅛ inch from the folded under edge to secure.

8 Take the backing piece with the larger folded flap – this is the button-hole piece. Fold in half lengthways and finger press to make a crease. Measure 2½ inches ether side of this crease and mark with a temporary fabric marker in the centre of the button-hole strip. Repeat at 7½ inches from the crease.

9 Using marks for placement, sew four button holes centred in the button-hole strip.

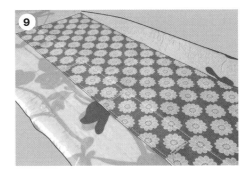

10 Lay this backing piece on top of the remaining backing piece, RSF, with button bands aligned. Mark through the button-holes on to the second backing piece for button placement.

**11** Attach buttons, either by hand or by machine.

**12** Button the two backing pieces together and lay, RST, with the pillow top. Pin securely all the way around the three pieces and sew together with a generous ¼-inch seam allowance. Trim any excess, zigzag or overlock the edges, turn through, and press.

## Tip
This is a great project for using up charm squares and little scraps. You don't need much fabric for EPP, and even your smallest scraps can be put to good use.

**Tip**
Choose a busy colourful print for the central bird and pull eight colours that feature in the print for the remaining birds to create a harmonious colour palette.

# Feathered Friends Pillow

This pillow puts a modern twist on the classic darting birds block, creating a flock of nine beautiful feathered fabric friends.

##  Materials

- BKG: ½ yd; Black Yarn Dyed
- Feature Print: 1 x FQ; Yellow floral
- Rect: 8 x 9 inches from each of eight colours
- Batting: 20 x 20 inches
- Lining: 20 x 20 inches
- Pillow back: 2 x (18½ x 12½ inches)
- Pillow insert: 18 inches sq

### Finished Measurements

- Approximately 18 inches square

## Instructions

1 Piece nine darting bird blocks following instructions in the block directory (see page 197).

 **Tip**
Cut pieces for all nine blocks before starting and chain piece the HSTs and four-patch sections.

2 Join blocks as a nine-patch.

3 Layer lining, batting and pillow top. Baste and quilt as desired. I quilted a grid, ¼ inch to both the left and right of each vertical and horizontal seam line.

4 Square up to 18½ inches.

5 Hem the backing pieces of the pillow by folding and pressing down ¼ inch on one long side. Repeat, and then top stitch to secure.

6 Lay pillow front right side down followed by both envelope back pieces right side up. Align raw edges of pillow front and back and pin securely.

7 Use the remaining feature print to bind the pillow as you would a quilt.

# Laptop Sleeve

A laptop sleeve is the perfect accessory for use at home or on the go. When you want to protect your laptop from scratches but don't want the bulk of a full case, look no further! The silky soft flannel on the inside will snuggle your laptop and protect it from even the slightest scratch.

## Materials

- Yellow fabric: 1 FQ
- Linen: 1 FQ
- Lining: 1 FQ flannel
- 10 x (2¾-inch) sqs
  (or as required for step three)
- Fusible fleece: ½ yd

## Finished Measurements

- Adjust to fit your laptop

## Instructions

1 Measure your laptop and make a note of the width, height and depth. For example, my 13-inch laptop is W: 12¼ inches x H: 8¾ inches x D: ¾ inch.

2 Work out the cutting size for your laptop sleeve following the simple formula below:
Height = W + D + 1 inch (14 inches for my case)
Width = H + D + 1 inch (10½ inches for my case).

3 Cut two lining pieces and two fusible fleece pieces at the size calculated.

4 Cut two strips from linen fabric measuring 2¾ inches x W. Piece the 10 sqs into two strips of five and join each to a linen fabric strip. Press to the linen. Note: If the patchwork strip is shorter than the linen strip, you will need to add another square.

5 Measure the height of your patchwork piece (A); it should be 5 inches. Cut main panels at width x (height – A + ½ inch). i.e. 10½ x 9½ inches.

6 Join main panel to patchwork panel. Press to the patchwork panel. Fuse to the fleece and quilt as desired.

7 Place main panel pieces RST and sew around side and bottom seams with a ¼-inch seam allowance. Repeat for lining leaving a turning gap in the bottom seam.

8 Place sleeve inside lining, RST. Sew all the way around the top seam. Clip corners to remove bulk.

9 Turn through, press well, and top stitch the top seam. Close turning hole with a slipstitch by hand or top stitch on the machine.

# Pincushions

A cute pincushion can make all the difference with your sewing projects. Well, not really, but you'll have fun making one. They make great gifts for sewing friends and prettify your sewing room.

## Little Liberty

## Instructions

**1** Lay squares as shown in diagram below and join together into rows. Press all seams open.

**2** Join rows to make the square. Press all seams open.

**3** Trim square by aligning the ⅜-inch mark on your ruler with the tips of the blue points. Trim all the way around.

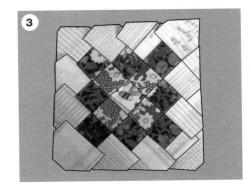

**4** Sew large BKG rectangles, RST, leaving a 1-inch gap in the centre of the seam for turning. Backstitch at either end of the opening. Press seam open.

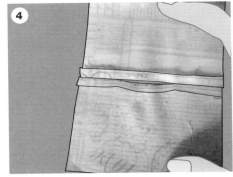

**5** Place pincushion front, RST, with the pincushion back centring the gap. Pin and sew all the way around the edge with a ¼-inch seam allowance.

**6** Clip corners, zigzag, or overlock the edges and turn through.

**7** Stuff the pincushion with fibrefill toy stuffing or rice as you desire. Hand stitch the opening closed using a ladder stitch.

## Materials

- Materials (All Liberty prints)
  White: 1 x (1-inch) sq
  Red: 4 x (1-inch) sqs
  Blue: 8 x (1-inch) sqs
- BKG: 12 x (1-inch) sqs,
  2 x (3 x 2½ inches)
- Fibrefill toy stuffing/rice

## Finished Measurements

- 2¼ inches square

# Spinning Spools

## Instructions

**1** Pair spool and BKG 1½-inch sqs and join to make 16 HSTs. Trim to 1 inch.

**2** Arrange all pieces for one spool block and join as a nine-patch. Press seams open. Repeat for each spool block. If you are using a directional print for the thread, check it is running across the spool.

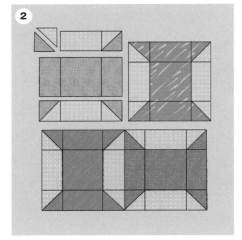

**3** Arrange four spool blocks as shown and join as a four-patch. Press seams open.

**4** Sew 2 (2½ x 4½-inch) BKG rects, RST, leaving a 2-inch gap in the centre of the seam for turning. Backstitch at either end of the opening. Press seam open.

**5** Place pincushion front, RST, with the pincushion back centring the gap. Pin and sew all the way around the edge with a ¼-inch seam allowance.

**6** Clip corners, zigzag or overlock the edges and turn through.

**7** Stuff the pincushion with fibrefill toy stuffing or rice as you desire. Hand stitch the opening closed using a ladder stitch.

 ## Materials

- Thread: Running stitch – Lush by Patti Young; 4 x (1½-inch) sqs
- Spool: Woodgrain – Aviary 2 by Joel Dewberry; 8 x (1 x 1½-inch) rects, 8 x (1½-inch) sqs
- BKG: Polka Dot Sewing Words – Riley Blake; 8 x (1 x 1½ inch) rects, 8 x (1½-inch) sqs, 2 x (2½ x 4½-inch) rects
- Fibrefill toy stuffing/rice

## Finished Measurements

- 4 inches square

# Giant Hexie

## Instructions

**1** Cut 6 strips from scraps: 5 x 1 inch x 3 inch and 1 x 1 inch x 2 inch.

**2** Sew one of the strips to one side of the centre hexie. Press seam away from centre.

**3** Line up the 60-degree mark on your ruler with the seam line just made and trim the strip to shape.

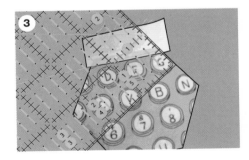

**4** Repeat for the other side.

**5** Take the next strip and sew to the next adjacent side. Trim as in step three.

**6** Repeat around the hexagon.

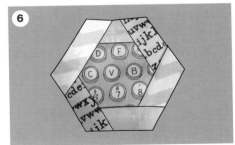

## Materials

- Centre hexie: 1½-inch sides using template on page 186
- Assorted scraps for rings
- Fusible fleece: 7 inches sq
- BKG: 2 x (5 x 7-inch) rects
- 2 co-ordinating ¾-inch buttons
- 1 yd co-ordinating ric rac braid
- Fibrefill toy stuffing/rice

## Finished Measurements

- 6 inches square

**7** Repeat for a further three rings. The strips should all be 1 inch in width but longer for each ring. Lengths should be as follows: round 2 = 3 inch, round 3 = 4 inch, round 4 = 5 inch.

**8** Use pincushion top as a template to cut out a hexagon of fusible fleece. Fuse to the back of pincushion top and quilt as desired. I used co-ordinating Aurifil thread and sewed a line down the middle of each ring.

**9** Baste ric rac braid on to pincushion top so that the peaks of the ric rac meet the edge of the hexagon.

**10** Take BKG pieces, join on the 7-inch side with a ¼-inch seam, leaving a 2-inch gap for turning. Backstitch at either end of the opening. Press seam open.

**11** Place pincushion front, RST, with the pincushion back centring the gap. Pin and sew all the way around the edge with a ¼-inch seam allowance. Trim the pincushion back to match the front.

**12** Clip corners, zigzag or overlock the edges and turn through.

**13** Stuff the pincushion with fibrefill toy stuffing or rice as you desire. Hand stitch the opening closed using a ladder stitch.

**14** Using a strong thread, take a few stitches through the centre of the pincushion to cinch it in.

**15** Hand stitch a button in the centre of the dimple on either side of the pincushion.

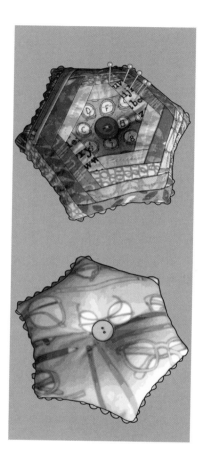

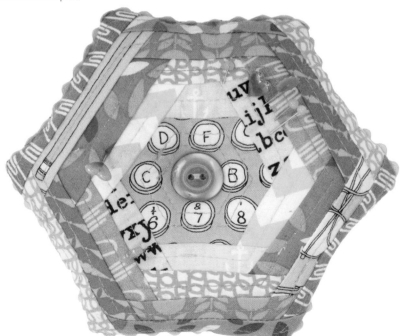

# Seaglass Quilt

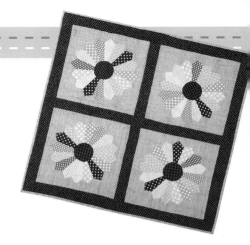

A Dresden Plate is one of my favourite shapes in quilting. Using a selection of colours and textures with a beach or nautical feel makes this perfect for a new baby boy. However, you could easily switch-up the fabrics to make this more feminine. Baby quilts are a great way of practising skills because they don't require a huge time investment.

## Materials

- 8 x F8ths: polka dot fabrics in
  Dark purple,
  Light purple,
  Dark blue,
  Light blue,
  Dark green,
  Light green,
  Lemon yellow,
  Mustard yellow
- BKG: 4 x (15-inch) sqs;
  Moda Cross Weave in Natural
- Border fabric: 6 x (2½ inches x
  WOF) strips and 4 x (5-inch) sqs;
  Sevenberry Dot in Navy
- Backing: 1 yd; Cosmo Cricket –
  Snorkel – Life Savers in Mint Julep.
  Note: This quilt only just fits on
  1 yd of backing, if you like a little
  more breathing room, buy 1¼ yds
- Binding: 4 x (2½ inches x WOF)
  strips; Tula Pink – The Birds and
  the Bees – Swallow Skies in
  Apple
- Freezer paper: 5 inches sq
- Dresden Plate (see page 211)

## Finished Measurements

- 35 inches square

## Instructions

1 Using the dresden template on page 185, cut eight leaves from each of the eight polka dot fabrics, 64 leaves total.

2 Fold dresden leaves in half lengthways, RST, and sew a ¼-inch seam along the top edge. Clip corner at the fold edge to reduce bulk when folded. Press at this folded stage to create a crease down the centre of the leaf.

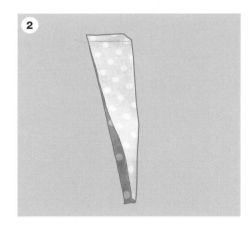

3 Turn dresden leaves out the right way and press the seam open using the tip of your iron. Use a turning tool or the tip of a pair of scissors to poke out the point when pressed.

4 Centre the seam on the central crease as created in step two; press to create the pointed edge.

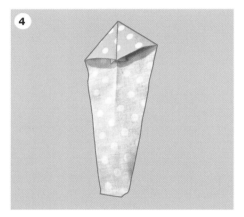

5 Arrange in four groups of 16 leaves. Join 16 leaves together using a ¼-inch seam to make a circle. Press all seams in same direction so that they spiral around.

## Tip

When sewing the dresden leaves together, match up the top pointed edges and sew from there down to the centre. It is important that the top edges match perfectly; the bottom edges will be covered up.

**6** Draw around a glass or mug on to the paper side of a piece of freezer paper to create a circular template. Choose a size that appeals to you, but make sure it covers the hole in the centre of the dresden – an approximately 3-inch diameter works well.

**7** Iron the waxy side of the template on to one square of border fabric. Trim edges ½ inch away from the circle. Using a long basting stitch, sew all the way around the edge of the shape, ¼ inch from the edge.

## Tip

This is easiest to do by hand, but you can use stitch length five on the sewing machine. Just remember not to backstitch.

**8** Holding on to one end of the thread, pull the other end to create a ruffle. Continue pulling and shuffling the fabric around so that the edges are cinched in over the template. Press well.

**9** Remove freezer paper and pin down on to the dresden plate. Appliqué using your chosen method; I used a small blanket stitch on my sewing machine in matching thread. Once appliquéd, trim excess dresden leaves on the reverse ½ inch from the appliqué seam line. Be very careful not to cut the centre.

**10** Fold the background sqs in to quarters and press to create a centre fold. Align the points of each dresden with these folds to centre on the background square. Pin well and appliqué as desired; I chose to edge stitch ⅛ inch from the edge using the sewing machine.

**11** Cut one of the border strips in half and use to sash the blocks into two pairs. Trim the excess. Use a further border strip to sash the blocks together into a four-patch. Trim again. Use the remaining four border strips to apply borders to the quilt top. Add the left and right borders first, trim, and then add the top and bottom.

**12** Baste, quilt and bind as desired. I quilted this using a FMQ stipple pattern in the background and straight line quilting for the dresden plate. I wanted to emphasise the spikey shape of the dresden and make it look a little more like a sea anemone. To do this, start ¼ inch from the centre circle in the seam between two leaves. Travel up to meet the point of the leaf, pivot, and come back down to ¼ inch from the centre circle in the seam between the next two leaves.

See Dresden Block in Block Directory on page 211.

# Baby Steps Quilt

There is nothing more luxurious than a flannel-backed voile quilt. It has that little something extra that turns a simple baby quilt into a beautiful heirloom. Voile is a bit trickier to work with than quilting weight cotton, but this pattern will help you find your feet.

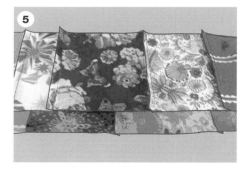

## Materials

- 14 x WOF strips in the following widths: 3 x 6 inches, 4 x 5 inches, 4 x 4 inches, 3 x 3 inches
- All 14 fabrics used are by one of my favourite designers, Anna Maria Horner. Her collections blend seamlessly together so that you can use prints from five different collections as I have done here, and still achieve a cohesive look to your quilt.
- Backing: 3 yds flannel
- Binding: 5 x (2½ inches x WOF) strips

## Finished Measurements

- 33 x 56 inches square

## Instructions

1 Arrange the strips in the following layout (the number indicates the width of strip): 6, 3, 4, 5, 3, 4, 5, 6, 5, 4, 3, 6, 4, 5.

2 Join all strips to make the top. Use a generous ¼-inch seam allowance and be very careful not to stretch the voile.

3 Join first and last strip of the quilt top, RST, to make a tube. Square up the edges, trimming any remaining selvedges.

4 Cut tube into 8 x 6-inch sections. Most voile is printed on 54-inch-wide base cloth; if yours is only 44 inches, you will only get six–seven sections, and this is fine.

### Tip

Use fabrics with high contrast in their values and patterns to create a bright and sharp look with this quilt.

5 Take one of the tube sections, find the point where the first and last fabrics meet, and carefully unpick that seam. Repeat for all other sections, unpicking the next seam along, i.e. first and second strip, second and third strip, third and fourth strip, etc.

6 Arrange sections in columns following the layout in the photograph. Join columns to make the quilt top.

7 Baste, quilt and bind as desired. I chose to do a FMQ loop-the-loop design. Because of the softness of the voile, the quilt can take a denser quilting without losing its drape.

**Tip**

When joining long strips of fabric, it is advisable to sew every row across the quilt in the opposite direction to the previous. Begin sewing the next strip at the point where you finished sewing the last. This will help prevent the quilt from warping in the middle.

# Liberty Style Wall Hanging

I love working with Liberty prints, even teeny tiny pieces because they feel so special. I made this wall hanging with my new sewing room in mind – I love how the disorganised nature of composition is made more cohesive through colour and scale, and I can't wait to hang it above my sewing machine for inspiration.

## Materials

- Liberty Prints in rainbow colours: 26 x (5-inch) sqs
- Hanging corners: 2 x (5-inch) sqs
- BKG: Linen x 1 FQ
- Backing: 1 FQ
- Binding: 2 x WOF strips
- Batting: 1 FQ
- Fusible web
- Spray baste

## Finished Measurements

- 17 x 19 inches

## Instructions

1 Using the templates on page 186, trace five large circles, 14 medium circles and seven small circles on to the paper side of your fusible web.

2 Divide the Liberty prints roughly into the following colours: Pink, Yellow/Orange, Green, Blue and Purple, and cut out the following shapes from each group:
Pink: one large, four medium
Yellow/Orange: three medium, four small
Green: two large, two medium, one small
Blue: one large, three medium
Purple: one large, two medium, two small.

3 Arrange circles following the layout in the image (or as desired) and fuse to the linen FQ following the instructions for your fusible web.

4 Baste wall hanging top on to the batting and backing using spray baste.

5 Using an appliqué stitch of your choice, such as zigzag or blanket, sew around the edge of each shape.

6 Press hanging corner sqs in half on the diagonal and pin to the back of the top left and right corners of the wall hanging. Bind as desired.

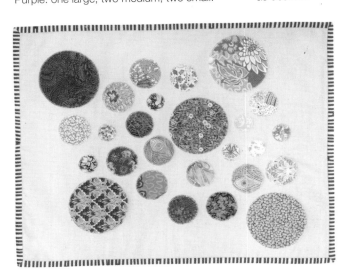

# Happy Picnic Table Runner

Runners are a really effective way of bringing a splash of colour to your dining table. They are quick to sew and make great gifts for family and friends. Incidentally, this runner also looks great in holiday print fabrics.

## Materials

- 40 x (4½-inch) sqs
- Lattice strips: 1 x FQ
- Batting: 16 x 37 inches
- Backing: 16 x 37 inches
- Binding: 3 x (2½ inches x WOF) strips
- Ruler: 6½ inches square
- Masking tape: 1 inch wide

## Finished Measurements

- 14 x 35 inches

## Instructions

1 Cut 40 x (4½-inch) squares. I used 20 different 10-inch squares and cut two squares from each with my die cutter.

2 Cut 40 x (1½ x 6-inch) strips from lattice fabric.

3 Cut all squares in half along the diagonal. Pair one triangle with one lattice strip, RST, and join with a ¼-inch seam allowance. Don't worry if the lengths aren't exactly the same at this point; the unit will be trimmed.

4 Repeat, joining second side of lattice strip with second triangle. Press.

5 Take a 3-inch piece of masking tape and mark the centre on the non-stick side at the top and bottom. Lay the tape on top of your square ruler starting at around the 1-inch mark and aligning the centre marks with the 45-degree line.

6 Trim squares to 4 inches using the tape to align with both sides of the lattice strip as shown. The tape mark will ensure you get a straight cut and that the centre of the lattice strip is centred in the block each time.

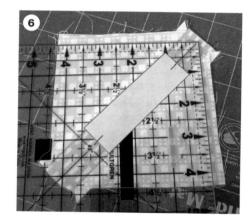

7 Arrange squares in four rows of 10. Join into rows, pressing seams in alternative directions. Then join rows to make the table runner.

8 Baste, quilt and bind as desired. I chose to quilt this in a loopy spiral FMQ design; the pattern is fairly geometric, but the fabric is floral and I wanted to soften the runner's look.

**Tip**
This pattern is really pre-cut friendly. It's perfect for your charm packs or layer cake squares.

# Potholders

Potholders are a great way of practising a new block or technique. They're quick to sew up and make cute housewarming gifts.

## Starburst Potholder

## Instructions

1 Pair together 3-inch BKG with 3-inch coloured sqs and join to make two HSTs. Trim to 2¼ inches. Repeat for all colours.

2 Sew together as a four-patch with BKG and 2¼-inch coloured sqs. Repeat for all colours.

3 Arrange four pieced sections from step two with BKG rects and centre sq. Sew together following the layout in the photograph.

4 Layer backing, binding, batting and then potholder. Baste and quilt as desired.

5 Press each pocket fabric in half to make a triangle, WST. Edge stitch ⅛ inch from folded edge. Pin to back of potholder. Square up block to 8½ inches, then round the corners using a glass or mug.

6 Press binding strip in half lengthways. Open out and press each edge in to meet the fold. Press in half again and sew ⅛ inch from the edge to secure.

7 Pin hanging loop to potholder following layout in diagram.

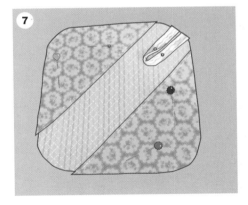

8 Bind potholder using WOF strip.

### Materials

- For each of four colours: 3-inch sqs, 2¼-inch sqs
- Centre: 1½ inches sq
- BKG: 4 x (3-inch) sqs, 4 x (2¼-inch) sqs, 4 x (1½ x 4-inch) rects
- Finger pockets: 2 x (6½-inch) sqs
- Binding: 2¼ inches x WOF strip, 2 x 6-inch rect
- Insulbrite: 10 inches sq
- Cotton batting: 10 inches sq
- Backing fabric: 10 inches sq

### Finished Measurements

- 8½ inches square

# Tulip Trivet

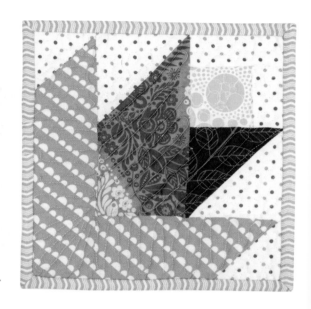

## Materials

- A: Yellow; 2½ inches sq
- B: Dark purple; 4 inches sq
- C: Light purple; 3½ x 6½-inch rect
- D: Green; 2½ x 6½-inch rect, 2½ x 8½-inch rect
- BKG: 2 x (2½-inch) sqs, 3½-inch sq, 4-inch sq, 1½ x 2½-inch small rect, 1½ x 3½-inch large rect
- Finger pockets: 2 x (6½-inch) sqs
- Binding: 2¼ inches x WOF strip, 2 x 6-inch rect
- Insulbrite: 10 inches sq
- Cotton batting: 10 inch sq
- Backing fabric: 10 inch sq

## Finished Measurements

- 8½ inches square

## Instructions

1 Join A and small BKG rect. Sew large BKG rect to top of this unit.

2 Pair B with 4-inch BKG sqs and join to make HSTs. Trim to 3½ inches. Join one HST to bottom of step one unit. Put the other HST aside for another project.

3 Add BKG 3½-inch sqs as CST to C rect. Join to RHS of step two unit. Trim excess and press.

4 Add BKG 2½-inch sqs as CSTs to both D rects. Trim excess. Join short rect to bottom of step three unit, followed by longer rect to LHS.

5 Continue as from step four of Starburst Potholder, without rounding the corners.

See Tulip Block in Block Directory on page 205.

## Tip

If you have a Teflon foot for your sewing machine, it may be easier to sew this top stitching with the lining facing you. If you don't, you will need to gently tug the bag through the sewing machine feed because the oilcloth grips to the throat plate more than regular cotton would; or place a sheet of tissue paper on top of the oilcloth to prevent it sticking.

# Snack Sack

Oilcloth, or coated cotton, is such a fun fabric to work with and makes for the perfect wipe-clean lunch bag. Be careful not to touch the plastic coating with an iron, and use a Teflon foot on your sewing machine for easier stitching.

## Materials

- 34 x (3½-inch) sqs; Color me Retro by Jeni Baker for Art Gallery Fabrics
- Red fabric: 2 x (2 x 12½-inch) strips, 2 x (2 x 3½-inch) rects, 2 x (1¼ x 15-inch) strips
- 1-inch cotton twill tape: 2 x (15-inch) lengths
- Oilcloth lining: 12½ x 22½-inch rect, 2 x (3½ x 11-inch) rects
- Fusible fleece: 12½ x 24½-inch rect, 2 x (3½ x 11-inch) rects

## Finished Measurements

- 11 x 12 x 3 inches

## Instructions

1 Arrange squares into seven rows of four and join to make a large rectangle. Sew remaining squares into two rows of three squares.

2 Join longer 2-inch red strips to either end of large rectangle. Join shorter 2-inch red strips to one end of each smaller rectangle.

3 Fuse patchwork pieces to fusible fleece and quilt as desired.

4 Beginning at the top of the bag, pair one side piece with main panel. Sew the length using a ¼-inch seam, and stop sewing ¼ inch before the end. Repeat with all side seams.

5 Squish the base of the bag together with the base of the side panel and sew using a ¼-inch seam. Press well to create creases in the shape of a box on the bag base.

6 Repeat steps four and five for the lining pieces, but there is no need to press.

7 Take remaining red fabric strips and press in half, WST, lengthways. Press raw edges in to meet the fold and press flat. Centre along cotton twill tape handles and pin to secure. Top stitch along both sides using an ⅛-inch seam allowance.

8 Position handles on main bag as shown in the picture and pin in place.

9 Place bag inside lining, RST. Pin at side seams. Sew all the way around the bag, leaving a 3-inch gap for turning. Turn through, press, and top stitch around the top of the bag.

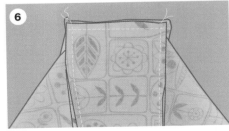

# Pinwheel Pouch

Zip pouches are one of my favourite things to sew because they are quick, useful and make great gifts. You may not realise it now, but you definitely need more zip pouches in your life. You can turn any quilt block into a zip pouch following the directions given below.

## Materials

- BKG: Navy; 2 x (3⅞-inch) sqs, 2 x (4¼-inch) sqs, 9½-inch sq
- Purple: 2 x (4¼-inch) sqs
- Lime: 1 x (4¼-inch) sq
- Aqua: 2 x (3⅞-inch) sqs
- Lining: 2 x (9½-inch) sqs
- Fusible fleece: 2 x (9½-inch) sqs
- Zip: 10 inches

## Finished Measurements

- 9 inches square

## Instructions

1 Sub cut all 3⅞-inch sqs once and all 4¼-inch sqs twice across the diagonal to yield triangles.

2 Join lime triangle with small BKG triangle to form larger triangle. Press seams open and trim doggy ears.

Pair this unit with aqua triangle to make a square. Repeat to make four squares.

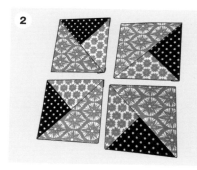

3 Join four squares to make a four-patch, following layout in the photo. Press seams open.

4 Sew one purple triangle to each side of the remaining small BKG triangles to form four triangle strips. Remember to offset the points by ¼ inch so the pieces align when pressed.

5 Lay out as per diagram and join triangle strips to each side of the centre square. Join large BKG triangles to block corners forming a square. Press block to form the pouch front.

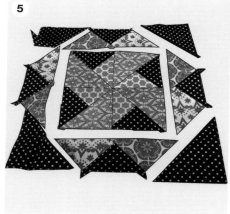

**6** Apply fusible fleece to front and back of pouch.

**7** Lay pouch front, WSF, aligned with top of pouch. Place lining, WSF, on top of that. Pin securely along the zip line.

**8** Using the zipper foot on your machine, sew the top seam line. Open out, press, and top stitch along this line.

**9** Place pouch back, RSF, zip (with other side of pouch attached) WSF, aligned with top of pouch and lining, WSF, on top of that. Pin securely along the zip line. Repeat step eight to sew the other side of the zip.

**10 IMPORTANT:** Open the zip at least halfway. Pair pouch front and back and lining front and back. Sew all the way around using a ¼-inch seam, and remember to leave a turning gap in the lining.

**11** Trim any excess zip, turn through, poke out corners and press well. Close the turning gap by hand with a slipstitch or top stitch on the machine.

# Christmas Bauble Baby Quilt

This is ideal for baby's first Christmas. Make this adorable little quilt for your own tiny addition to the family or give it as a gift that will be cherished forever.

## Materials

- 1 x charm pack Christmas fabrics: Moda – In from the Cold – Kate Spain
- 1 x charm pack white fabric: Moda – Bella solids
- Borders: 2 x (5 x 30 inches), 2 x (5 x 38 inches)
- Batting: 40 x 40 inches
- Backing: 1½ yds

## Finished Measurements

- 37 inches square

### Tip

This is the perfect project to make use of a die cutting machine. Any drunkards path die that finishes at 3½ inches can be used to cut the shapes.

## Instructions

Refer to block 15 in the block directory.

1 Separate four patterned charm squares and set aside for later. From the remaining patterned charm squares, using templates on page 188, cut 36 fans and 24 arches. From white charms, cut 36 arches and 24 fans.

2 Pair patterned arches and plain fans and join following the 'no pins curve' sewing technique. These instructions are repeated in the Blocks chapter too.

3 Repeat for all plain arches and patterned fans. Press all seams towards the arch.

4 Join patterned centre blocks into nine sets of four, as shown in the diagram, and sew into a nine-patch to create the centre of the quilt. Press seams open.

5 Join remaining blocks into four rows of six. Take the four charm squares set aside in step one and trim down to 4 inches. Join to either end of two of the rows.

6 Sew the short rows to the left and right of the quilt, followed by the longer rows to the top and bottom. Press seams open.

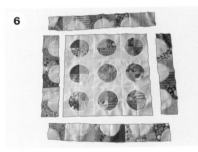

6

7 Sew short border strips to the left and right of the quilt, followed by the longer border strips to the top and bottom. Press seams towards the borders.

8 Baste, quilt and bind as desired. I chose to hand quilt in a chunky perle thread. I love the look of the thick red stitches against the white background.

# Obsession Quilt

You will find, as you get into quilting, some patterns just play on your mind and leave you with no room for anything else. This pattern did that for me. A conversation one night with my mum turned into this quilt less than three days later. Needless to say, I was obsessed!

## Materials

Approximately 16 FQs are needed to make this quilt top, although I used more colours for variety.

- BKG: assorted low-volume prints; 96 x (4½-inch) sqs, 48 x (5-inch) sqs
- Navy/Brown: 8 x (4½-inch) sqs
- Yellow: 48 x (4½-inch) sqs
- From each of
  Teal,
  Aqua,
  Lime,
  Orange,
  Light Pink,
  Magenta: 24 x (4½-inch) sqs, 8 x (5-inch) sqs
- Batting: 2½ yds
- Backing: 5 yds
- Binding: ¾ yd
- Note: Nearly all fabrics used in this quilt are by Art Gallery Fabrics.

## Finished Measurements

- 80 inches square

## Instructions

1 Pair all 5-inch coloured and BKG sqs. Join to make HSTs. Trim to 4½ inches sq.

2 Divide sqs and HSTs into four even piles. Take one pile and lay out all sqs in a 10 x 10 arrangement using the HSTs to form the edges of an 'X' as in the diagram.

3 Join into rows to form one quarter of the quilt. Repeat steps two and three for the remaining three piles of squares. Note: there is a flow of colour in the quadrants, going from pink to orange to yellow to lime to aqua. The low-volume prints are backgrounds of the X.

4 Join quarters as a four-patch to form quilt top. Baste, quilt and bind as desired. I quilted this in concentric circles, 2 inches apart.

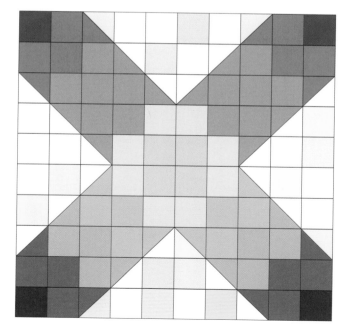

It can help to visualise a quilt pattern by drawing it out on paper or on the computer before you start cutting your fabric. I like to keep graph paper and some colouring pencils handy to doodle potential quilt patterns while I'm talking on the phone.

### Tip

When quilting concentric circles, starting off-centre like I did here is a good idea. It adds a touch of whimsy and interest to the quilt and can make for a real time saver. Once the circle is large enough to be broken by the edge of the quilt, there is no need to hide your thread ends anymore.

### Tip

Large scale prints work great on quilt backs. When a quilt has such a busy front, I like to use plain colours and simple prints for the back. A polka dot, a stripe or a simple text print like this one balances out all that colour.

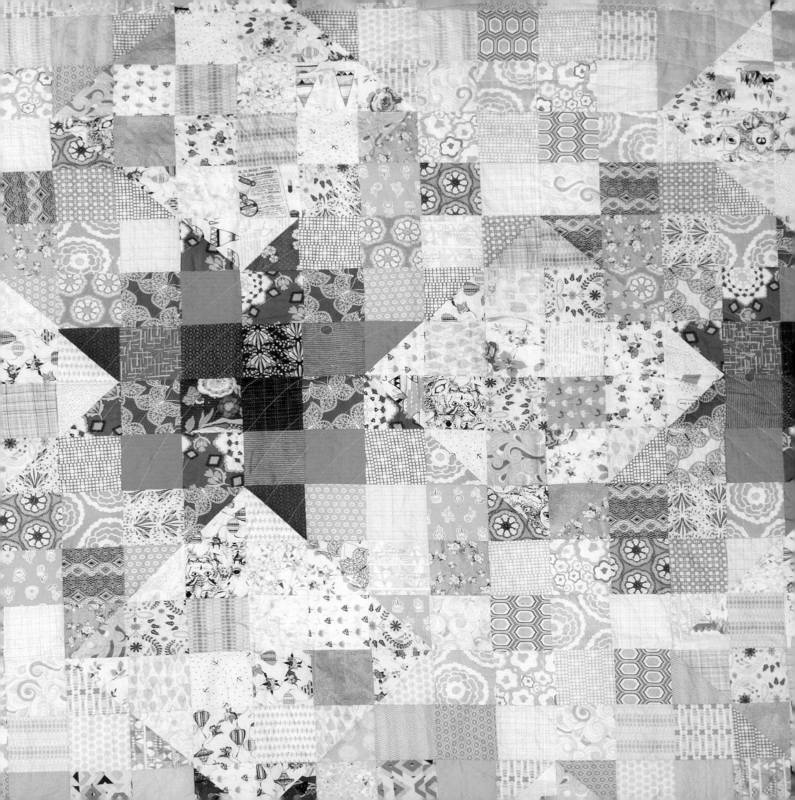

# His 'n' Hers Stockings

This is a really inexpensive project that makes use of selvedges, the printed edge of the fabric. If you don't save your selvedges, start now and maybe next year you'll have enough to make a whole family of stockings.

## Materials

Makes two stockings

- Approximately 40 selvedge strips in festive colours: red, green, blue
- Batting: 2 x (18 x 22-inch) rects
- Lining: 4 x (18 x 22-inch) rects
- Backing: 2 x (18 x 22 inch) rects
- Gingham bias binding: 3¼ yds
- Festive ribbon: 2 x (12-inch) lengths

## Finished Measurements

- 12 x 22 inches

## Instructions

1 Enlarge the stocking template on page 187 by 100 percent on to paper and cut out. Draw around it using a thick marker on to the batting to make an outline.

2 Collect your selvedge strips and arrange them to cover the outline. Starting with the bottom right corner, angle the selvedges and lay them over the template ensuring to overlap the previous strip by ⅛–¼ inch.

3 When the whole template is covered, collect the strips in order. Take the batting and the first two strips to the sewing machine. Overlap the strips and sew a line of stitching down the middle of the overlap that will secure both pieces.

### Tip

I used 12wt Aurifil thread here to give the stitches some definition. When working with a thicker thread such as this, lengthen your stitches to at least 3.5.

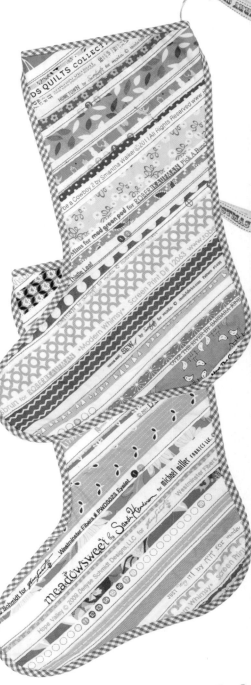

153

**4** When all selvedges have been sewn down, pin the paper template on to the front of the strip pieced section, and neatly cut out the stocking shape.

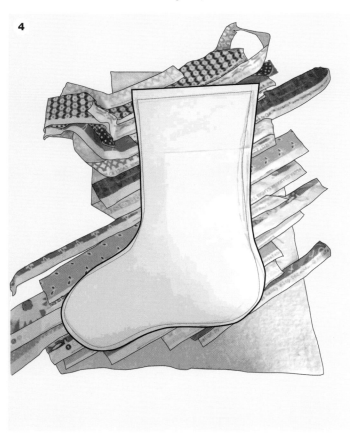

4

**5** For each stocking front, cut out a further two stocking shapes from the lining fabric, and one from the backing fabric. The backing and one of the lining pieces need to be a mirror image of the stocking front. Layer backing fabric RS down, lining fabric RST on top of that, followed by stocking front RS facing. Securely pin together and machine baste ⅛ inch from the edge around the outside edge of the stocking. Do not baste around the top of the stocking as this will be the opening.

**6** Attach bias binding to the front of the stocking sandwich using the sewing machine. Finish by hand on the reverse side.

**7** When the side binding is secure, apply binding to the outside edge of the top ring. Begin by folding ½ inch of the edge of the binding back on itself and pressing. Make sure to open the layers of the stocking so that the lining and front are on one side and the lining and back are on the other. Attach binding all the way around the ring, overlapping when you reach the start point.

**8** Hand stitch the binding to the inside to finish.

**9** Create a loop of ribbon by folding it in half and hand stitch to secure approximately 1 inch inside the stocking.

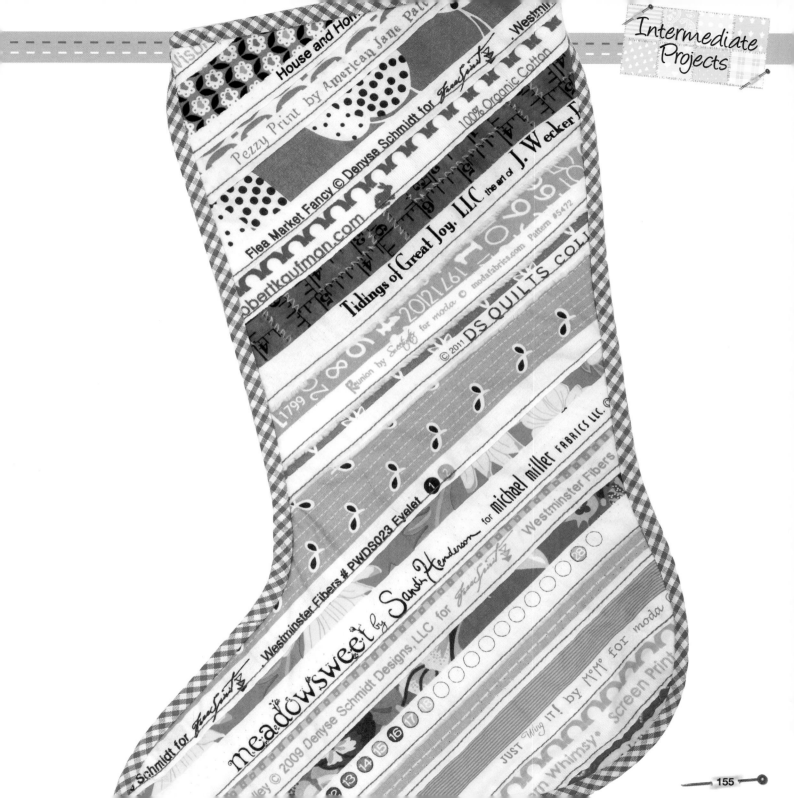

# Picnic Posy Quilt

Thirties style reproduction prints give a really cute and rustic feel to any quilt. I especially love using them in a traditional block such as a log cabin for a cosy homemade look.

## Materials

Approximately 12 FQs are needed to make this quilt top, although I used more colours for variety.

- Red: 12 x (2½-inch) sqs
- From assorted thirties style reproduction prints:
  12 x (2½-inch) sqs
  24 x (2½ x 4½-inch) rects
  24 x (2½ x 6½-inch) rects
  24 x (2½ x 8½-inch) rects
  24 x (2½ x 10½-inch) rects
  24 x (2½ x 12½-inch) rects
  12 x (2½ x 14½-inch) rects
- 100 percent cotton batting: 12 x (16-inch) sqs
- Backing: 2 yds x 60-inch-wide red 1-inch gingham print
- Binding: 6 x (2½ inches x WOF) strips
- Red perle cotton

## Finished Measurements

- 42 x 56 inches

## Instructions

**1** Sort fabric pieces into 12 piles. Make 12 log-cabin blocks following the QAYG instructions on page 72. I like to have between two and three lines of quilting on each log.

**2** Square up blocks to 14½-inch square. Join into four rows of three, then join rows using a ¼-inch seam to form quilt top. Press seams open using a hot steam iron.

**3** Baste quilt front on to backing, then quilt into the ditch between all blocks.

**4** Using perle cotton, tie the quilt in the middle of each block.

**5** Bind as desired.

See Log Cabin Block in Block Directory on page 196.

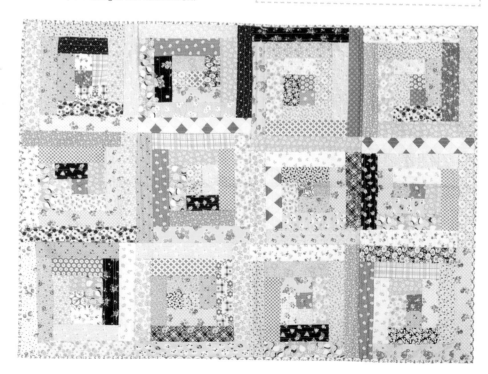

# Chum Dashing

This mini churn dash quilt shows you that sometimes, too much colour is a great thing. Go crazy with your fabric choices here; the more the merrier. The neons paired with black and white create enough contrast for the shapes to stand out, but this quilt would look equally fabulous in softer vintage floral designs and ticking stripes too.

## Materials

- Churn dashes: assorted scraps. If working from stash, 2 x FQs are sufficient to make 12 x (6-inch) finished blocks.
- Batting: 64 inches sq
- Backing: 4 yds; black on white polka dot
- Binding: ½ yd; white on black pixie dot

## Finished Measurements

- 60 inches square

## Instructions

**1** Make 100 x (6-inch) finished churn dash blocks referring to the block directory on page 201 for directions and working to the following piece measurements:
BKG: 2 x (3-inch) sqs, 4 x (1½ x 2½-inch) rects, 2½-inch sq.
Churn: 2 x (3-inch) sqs, 4 x (1½ x 2½-inch) rects.

**2** Join blocks into 25 four-patches. Arrange larger blocks in a five by five layout and join rows to make the quilt top.

**3** Baste, quilt and bind as desired. I chose to quilt this in a larger scale FMQ stipple pattern; with so many small pieces, I wanted the quilting to blend into the background and not detract from the fabrics.

See Churn Dash Block in Block Directory on page 201.

# Sew and Go Tote

This tote is quick to make and perfect for Saturday morning trips to the market, afternoons with sewing friends, or just to carry all your day-to-day stuff in. The fold-over top and canvas bottom are cute design features, but it's the fabric that really sings for me in this project.

## Materials

- Assorted coloured fabrics (bright, Japanese-style prints): 16 x (5-inch) sqs
- Assorted BKG fabrics (low volume prints): 16 x (5-inch) sqs
- Heavyweight canvas: 2 x (4½ x 16¼-inch) rects
- Lining fabric A: 2 x (16¼-inch) sqs
- Lining fabric B: 2 x (4½ x 16¼-inch) rects
- Heavyweight cotton twill tape: 2 x (52-inch) lengths
- Fusible fleece: 2 x (16¼-inch) sqs

## Finished Measurements

- 16 x 20 inches

# Instructions

1 Pair all the 5-inch coloured and BKG sqs together. Join to make HSTs. Trim to 4½-inch sqs.

2 Arrange HSTs into two large squares of 16 HSTs and join as a 16-patch. Apply fusible fleece to the reverse of each panel following manufacturers directions.

3 Join canvas strips to the bottom of each panel and press seams towards the canvas. Top stitch ⅛ inch from either side of seam.

4 Lay one piece of twill tape on top of the other, pin down the length, and join by sewing ⅛ inch from the edge down both sides.

5 Making sure that the strap is not twisted, pin each end to the side of one panel. Align the top of the straps with the seam line between the first and second row of HSTs. The raw edges should stick out over the edge of the panel by approximately 1 inch.

6 Pair panels, RST, and sew all the way around three sides, leaving the top open. Backstitch over the straps in the side seams for reinforcement. Press seams open.

**7** Box the corners of the outer bag by pinching together each side and bottom seam until they meet and form a triangle at the point. Pin this securely, measure, and mark 2 inches from the corner point.

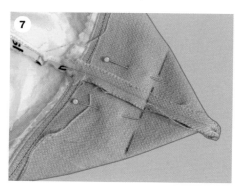

Sew along this line, backstitching at each end, then cut off the excess corner ¼ inch from the sewn line. Repeat for each corner.

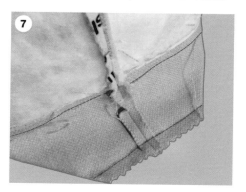

**8** Repeat steps three, six and seven for the lining fabric. When joining the lining panels together, leave a 4-inch turning gap in the bottom seam.

**9** Place outer bag inside bag lining, RST. Pin at side seams and sew all the way around the top. Turn through, press well, and top stitch ⅛ inch from the top of the bag. Slipstitch or top stitch the turning gap to finish.

**10** Press the top of the bag over into its natural folded position. Use steam and press a number of times to form a neat crease.

**Tip**
Before cutting the excess, turn the outer bag to check the boxed corner, it's much easier to adjust before you cut.

# Postcards from Japan Wall Hanging

I've always been inspired by and interested in Japanese culture, more recently through their fabrics. This flower shape is inspired by the cherry blossom, and the little snippets of fabric pay homage to the Japanese kawaii (meaning cute) designs.

## Materials

- 24 x (5-inch) sqs assorted scraps
- BKG: ½ yd
- Backing: ½ yd
- Batting: 18 x 26 inches
- Binding: 2 x (2½ inches x WOF) strips
- Hanging corners: 2 x (5-inch) sqs

## Finished Measurements

- 16 x 24 inches

## Instructions

**1** Make 24 copies of the template on page 185 and foundation piece 24 segments. The numbers on the template refer to the order in which you sew them together. Refer to the foundation paper piecing techniques on page 60. Join four flower segments as a 4-patch to make six full flower shapes.

**2** Join blocks into a two by three layout.

**3** Baste and quilt as desired. I quilted this with a large-scale diagonal crosshatch.

**4** Before binding, press the two hanging corners in half, WST, to make triangles. Pin into place aligning with the top left and right corners on the reverse of the wall hanging.

**5** Bind as desired.

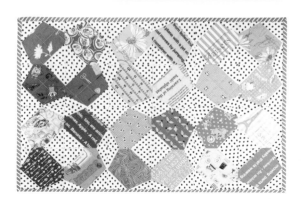

# Welcome Home Pillow

The Courthouse Steps block is an age-old favourite. Accurate piecing and forward planning is key with this project. Pillows are a great way to practice hand quilting because the reverse is hidden inside.

## Materials

- Black: 2 x 18-inch strip
- Assorted Fat 8ths: 24 different prints (4 x Light Green, 4 x Dark Green, 5 x Light Blue, 5 x Navy, 6 x White)
- Batting: 25 inches sq
- Backing: 22 x 23 inches
- Zip-flap: 4 x 22 inches
- Zip: 22 inches
- Pillow insert: 20 inches

## Finished Measurements

- Approximately 22 inches square

## Instructions

1 Piece nine courthouse step blocks following instructions in block directory (see page 198), working to the following piece measurements.
Centre: 2 inches sq
1½-inch-wide strips cut to the following lengths:
Top and bottom:
2 x (1½ x 2 inches), 2 x (1½ x 4 inches), 2 x (1½ x 6 inches)
Left and right:
2 x (1½ x 4 inches), 2 x (1½ x 6 inches), 2 x (1½ x 8 inches)

2 Sew blocks together as a nine-patch. Press seams open.

3 Baste and quilt as desired. I opted to hand quilt a 3-inch diamond in each of the smaller sections, and a 4-inch diamond in each of the larger.

4 Trim pillow front to 22 inches square.

5 Cut backing fabric in half to form 2 x (22 x 11½-inch) rects.

6 Press zip-flap fabric in half along the length, WST.

6

**7** Match raw edges of zip-flap with long edge of one background rect, RST. Lay zip on top, WSF with zip pull on the right. Pin along length of edge.

**8** Attach zipper foot to machine, and sew through all three layers very close to the zip teeth.

 Tip
When you are about 5 inches from the end, stop, leaving the needle down. Lift up presser foot and unzip the zip. Wiggle the zip pull up past the presser foot and continue sewing.

**9** Press flap over zip and top stitch ⅛ inch from the seam to secure.

**10** Pin raw edge of zip, RST, with remaining backing rect.

**11** Sew through two layers with zipper foot, very close to the teeth.

**12** Press backing fabric away from the zip and top stitch ⅛ inch from the seam to secure.

**13** Unzip the zip at least halfway. You may find it useful to pin or bar-tack across the top of the zip to hold the two backing rects together.

**14** Place pillow front and backing RST, pin all the way around the edge and sew together with a generous ¼-inch seam allowance.

**15** Finish raw edges with zigzag or overlocking stitch. Clip corners, turn through, and press.

 Tip
Start with a simple sketch and use colouring pencils to plan your fabric placement.

# Honeycomb Table Centre

This project uses the really fun method of quilt-as-you-go hexies. They can be entirely hand sewn if desired, but I like the added detail of the stitching line on the reverse of the project.

## Materials

- 19 x (6½-inch) sqs
- 19 x (4-inch) sqs
- Batting: 19 x (4-inch) sqs
- Stiff cardboard for templates
- (Fabrics shown: Glimma by Lotta Jansdotta for Windham Fabrics)

## Finished Measurements

- Approximately 12 x 28 inches

## Instructions

**1** Transfer hexagon templates from page 184 to stiff card and cut out 19 large and 19 small hexagons from fabric, and 19 small hexagons from batting.

**2** Centre small hex and batting, RS facing, on top of the large hexagon, RS down. Pin into place.

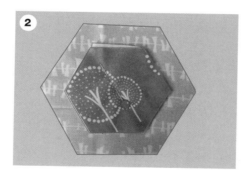

**3** Begin by pressing one side of the large hex in to meet the small hex. Fold and press again so that the raw edge is now enclosed.

**4** Repeat the double fold on the adjacent side,
securing with a pin or clip once folded.
Repeat around the hex.

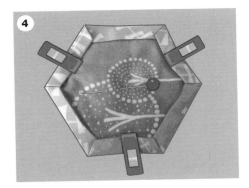

**5** Sew around the hex, as close to the edge of
the fold as possible.

**6** Arrange hexagons in layout as shown and
sew by hand using ladder stitch to join.
Alternatively, use a decorative or zigzag
machine stitch.

# Cityscape Table Mats

Individual table mats can bring a fresh look to your dining area. Using the same fabric, similar geometric style and similar quilting ties these two mats together whilst retaining their unique designs.

## Materials

- 1 x charm pack; Collage by Such Designs for Windham Fabrics
- Natural linen: ½ yd
- Backing: ½ yd; Australia Spotlight News Print
- Fusible fleece: 2 x (14 x 16-inch) rects

## Finished Measurements

- Approximately 13 x 15 inches

## Instructions

### Mat One (Brick Wall)

1 Choose 13 charm squares and cut in half to form 13 x (2½ x 5-inch) rects. Choose four charm squares and cut into quarters to form 4 x (2½-inch) sqs. Reserve the remaining fabric for the second place mat.

2 Cut 4 x (1 inch x WOF) strips from the linen. Sub-cut the strips into the following lengths: 6 x (14-inch), 2 x (13-inch), 12 x (2½ inch).

3 Use the shortest strips to sash the rectangles and squares together in a brick arrangement as shown. Use the longest strips to sash the horizontal rows together. Use the remaining strips to sash the left and right side of the place mat.

### Mat Two (Dash Dot)

1 Choose 10 charm squares and cut in half to form 10 x (2½ x 5-inch) rects. Choose five charm squares and cut into quarters to form 5 x (2½-inch) sqs. Reserve the remaining fabric for the first place mat.

2 Cut 4 x (1 inch x WOF) strips from the natural linen. Sub cut the strips into the following lengths: 4 x (12-inch), 2 x (15-inch), 10 x (2½-inch). Cut a further two rects from natural linen, 1⅞ x 12 inches, 2⅜ x 12 inches.

3 Use the shortest strips to sash two rectangles to either side of one square. Arrange in layout shown using the 12-inch strips to separate the columns. Sew together.

4 Sash the left and right with 12-inch strips, and the top and bottom with the 15-inch strips.

### For Both Mats:

1 Fuse the fleece to the reverse of the mat following manufacturer's directions.

2 Baste, quilt and bind as desired. Since drape is not important with this project and they will always be flat on a table, I chose to use very heavy quilting in an organic straight-line pattern.

Brick Wall

Dash Dot

# Laptop Case

In my experience, you can never have too many laptop cases. This is a fun pattern to introduce you to curved zip installation. Once you've mastered the process, try embellishing the front of the laptop case in your own patchwork style.

 ## Materials

- Purple fabric: 1 FQ
- Grey fabric: 1 FQ
- Lining: 1 FQ
- Fusible fleece: ½ yd
- Zip: 24 inches or 6 inches longer than width measurement calculated below

## Finished Measurements

- Adjust to fit your laptop

## Instructions

1 Measure your laptop and make a note of the width, height and depth. For example, my 13-inch laptop is W: 12¼ inches, H: 8¾ inches, D: ¾ inch.

2 Work out the cutting size for your laptop case following the simple formula below: Width = W + D + 1½ inches (14½ inches for my case) and H = H + D + 1½ inches (11 inches for my case).

3 Cut two lining rects and four fusible fleece rects at the size calculated.

4 Divide height measurement roughly into one quarter vs three quarters, eg. for 11 inches, 8 inches (A) and 3 inches (B). Cut main panel pieces (A + ½ inch) x Width; cut contrast panel pieces (B + ½ inch) x Width. So for my case it would be, 8½ x 14½ inches and 3½ x 14½ inches.

5 Join main and contrast panel pieces with a ¼-inch seam. Press seam open.

6 Fuse main panels and lining pieces to fusible fleece. Quilt or top stitch main pocket pieces if desired.

7 Position zip centred along top edge of one main panel piece. It should extend approximately 3 inches down either side. If the zip is too long, cut from the base of the zip and make a fabric zip stopper. To do this, take a 1½ x 2-inch piece of fabric and press in half lengthways. Press raw edges in to meet in the middle; then enclose end of zip in fold. Top stitch slowly and carefully.

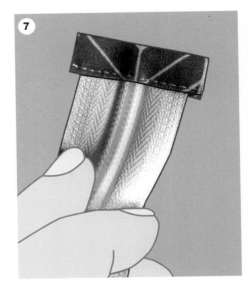

7

**8** Pin zip, WSF, along length of top edge. When you get to the corner, clip small notches into the zip tape every ¼ inch. This will allow it to easily make a curve. Curve around the corner and pin in place.

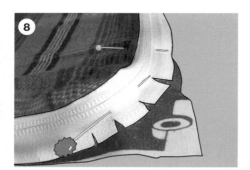

**9** Using the zipper foot on your sewing machine, join the zip to the main pocket panel. Start sewing ½ inch after the beginning of the zip and stop ½ inch before the end. Remove pins.

**10** Lay lining panel WSF on top of main panel. Match bottom corners and pin in place on top of the zip. Flip sandwich over so that the WS of main panel is showing, and sew along the previous stitch line to catch the lining.

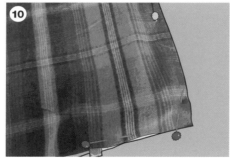

**11** Trim excess fabric from around curve and clip notches into seam allowance. Turn RS out and press. Top stitch carefully along length of zip.

**12** Lay remaining main pocket panel RSF, and position the sewn main panel face down on top. Repeat steps eight–eleven to attach zip and lining to second main panel.

**13** Turn so all pieces are RS out, then, IMPORTANT, open the zip. Turn so that the lining is showing. Flip back the lining pieces so they are out of the way and sew the main panel bottom seams using a ½-inch seam allowance. Extend the side seams ½ inch into the zip tabs to secure.

**14** Pull lining pieces even further back and sew the bottom seam using a ½-inch seam allowance and leaving a 4-inch gap for turning.

**15** Turn through, press well, and close gap with a slipstitch or top stitch to finish.

# Travel Sewing Kit

If you love EPP, you need a travel EPP case. Even if you're not travelling anywhere, this case is great to keep on the arm of the sofa so all the bits and pieces are at hand when you need them.

## Materials

- Liberty print: 58 x (2½-inch) sqs
- Batting: 12 x 14 inches
- Lining: 10 x 13 inches
- Zip: 7 inches
- Zip pocket: 4 x (4 x 10-inch) rects
- Thread pocket: 2 x (4 x 10-inch) rects
- Pocket binding: 2 x (2½ x 10-inch) strips
- Lightweight interfacing: 2 x (4 x 10-inch) rects, 2 x (3-inch) sqs, 10 x 13-inch rect
- Felt: 2 x (2½ x 4½-inch) rects (cut with pinking shears)
- EPP pocket: 2 x (3-inch) sqs
- Scissor strap: 1½ x 6-inch rect
- Silver lanyard hook clasp
- Ties: 1½ inches x WOF strip
- Binding: 2 x (2½ inches x WOF) strip
- 1-inch cotton twill tape: 3-inch strip

## Finished Measurements

- 10 x 13 inches (when open)

## Instructions

1 Make 58 EPP hexagons from template on page 186 and join into a rectangle formed of four rows of seven and five rows of six.

2 Press, remove papers and baste on to batting. Quilt as desired, then trim to 10 x 13 inches.

3 Fuse large interfacing rect to lining rect, smaller interfacing rects to thread pocket pieces, and interfacing sqs to paper pieces pocket sqs. Set all pieces aside.

4 On the reverse of one of the zip pocket pieces, mark a ½-inch rectangle, starting 1 inch down from the top edge and 2 inches in from either side. Draw a line down the centre of this rectangle, extending points into the corners. Place RST with another zip pocket piece, and sew around the rectangle. Cut along the line in the middle and snip into the corners, getting as close to the stitches as possible.

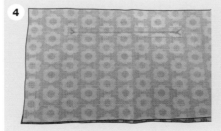

5 Push one side of the pocket piece through the hole. Wiggle the fabric to get a neat finish then press well.

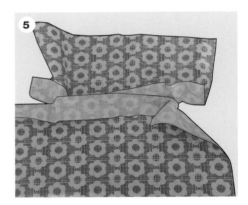

Pin zip so it shows through the rectangle, and top stitch into place.

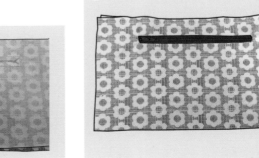

6 Place remaining zip pocket pieces WST. Lay zip pocket on top of remaining pieces and baste along the short edges, ⅛ inch from the edge.

7 Press both pocket binding pieces in half lengthways. Use one to bind top edge of zip pocket. Place thread pocket pieces WST and bind using the remaining binding piece.

8 Place EPP pocket pieces, WST, and sew around three sides. Clip bottom corners, turn through, and press. Turn opening ¼ inch inside pocket and press. Set aside.

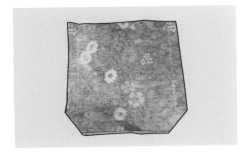

9 Lay thread pocket on left hand side of lining and zipper pocket on the right. Baste to lining ⅛ inch from the edge. Sew three separating lines onto the pocket as per photograph.

10 Position EPP pocket square and felt pieces in the center of the case to gauge position. Sew around three sides of the EPP pocket square, enclosing the open side and leaving the top open. Sew along the top edge of the felt pieces.

11 Lay cotton twill tape over top edge of felt pieces (optional – embellish twill tape with small fabric scrap). Sew around all four sides.

12 Press scissor strap in half lengthways, then press edges in to meet the fold. Press in half and sew down length. Repeat for ties.

13 Thread scissor strap through lanyard hook and pin in position as in main photograph.

14 Fold tie in half and pin to centre of one short edge of the case front. Baste lining on to case front, WST, ⅛ inch from the edge.

15 Machine stitch binding on to case with front side facing. Finish by hand on the inside.

Sewing kit can be folded in half or into thirds or tied with the ties to secure.

# Rock Around a Snowball Table Runner

Dressing the Christmas table with my mum is one of my favourite holiday traditions. This table runner is perfect for family gatherings, whatever size your table. You can make it smaller or longer by adding more of the ringed snowball blocks, or change the layout to make a square.

## Materials

- Rings and centres: 12 x Fat 8ths
- BKG: ½ yd
- Batting: 16 x 56 inches
- Backing: 16 x 56 inches
- Binding: 4 x (2½ inches x WOF) strips

## Finished Measurements

- 14 x 53 inches

## Instructions

1 Divide the 12 fabrics into four groups of three, choosing one fabric for the centre square, ring one and ring two for each of the four blocks.

2 Cut fabrics for each block following the measurements and cutting layout as follows:
Centre square: 6½ inches
Ring 1: 4 x (2½-inch) sqs, 2 x (2 x 6½-inch) short strips, 2 x (2 x 9½-inch) long strips
Ring 2: 4 x (3½-inch) sqs, 2 x (2 x 9½-inch) short strips, 2 x (2 x 12½-inch) long strips
BKG: 4 x (4½-inch) sqs

In addition you will also need:
BKG: 5 x (1½ x 12½-inch) short strips, 3 x (1½ inches x WOF) long strips.

3 Add ring one sqs to centre sq as CSTs.

4 Add ring one short strips to left and right of centre sq followed by long strips to top and bottom. Press and square to 9½ inches.

5 Repeat step three for ring two strips. Press and square to 12½ inches.

6 Add BKG sqs to block as CSTs.

7 Join blocks together using BKG short sashing strips and add a sashing strip to either end.

8 Sew BKG long strips together at the short ends to create one long strip. Use to sash the long edges of table runner.

9 Baste and quilt as desired. I chose a standard FMQ loopy stipple pattern to give the table runner some stability. No doubt it will need washing if used on our Christmas table.

10 Bind the runner. If using straight grain binding, you will need the four strips as stated above. If using bias strips, you will need approximately 170 inches.

**Tip**

Keep a stash of red and white striped fabric on hand; it makes the perfect candy cane stripe binding when cut on the bias.

# Templates

These are the templates used throughout this book. Most are true to size, so you just need to photocopy and use at your convenience to make amazing quilt after quilt.

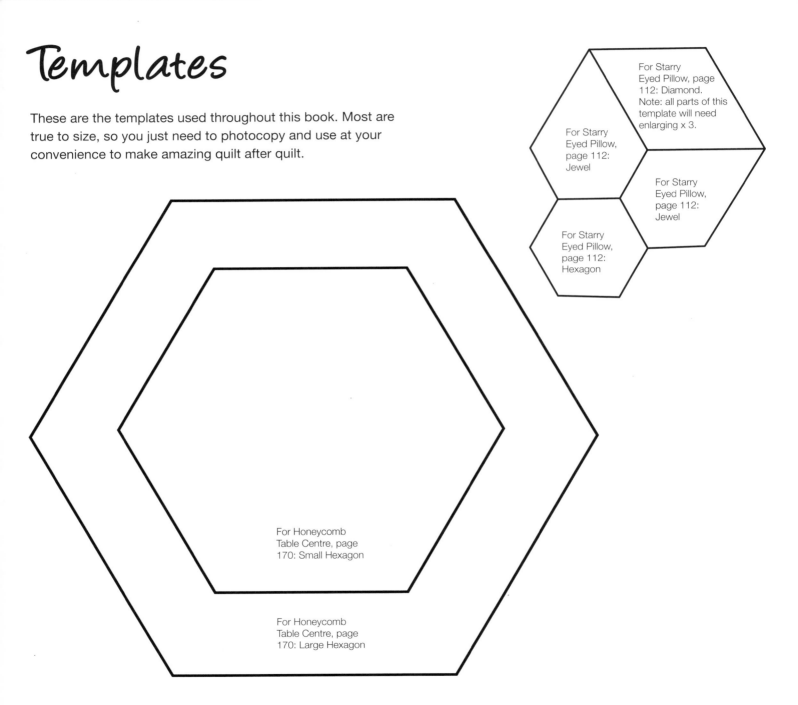

For Starry Eyed Pillow, page 112: Diamond. Note: all parts of this template will need enlarging x 3.

For Starry Eyed Pillow, page 112: Jewel

For Starry Eyed Pillow, page 112: Jewel

For Starry Eyed Pillow, page 112: Hexagon

For Honeycomb Table Centre, page 170: Small Hexagon

For Honeycomb Table Centre, page 170: Large Hexagon

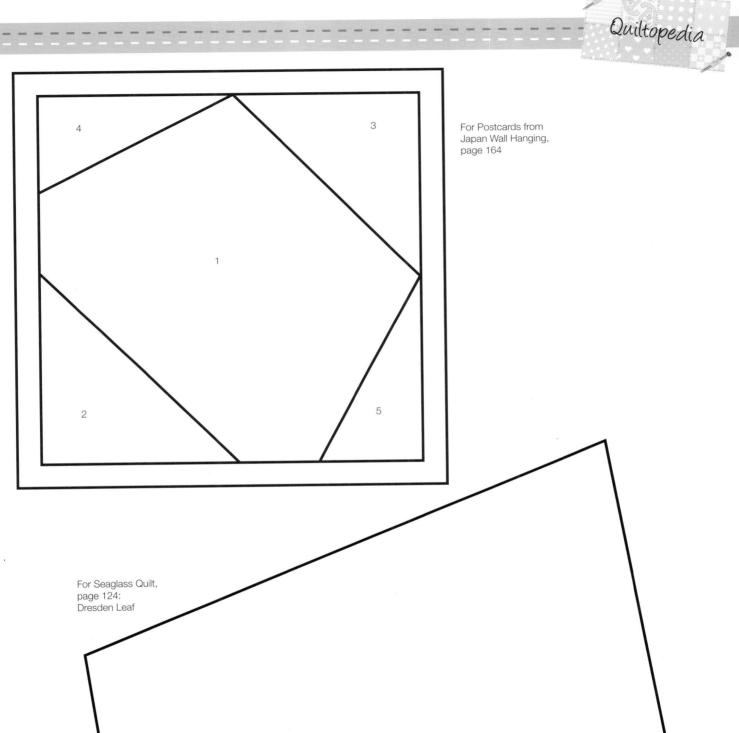

4

3

1

2

5

For Postcards from
Japan Wall Hanging,
page 164

For Seaglass Quilt,
page 124:
Dresden Leaf

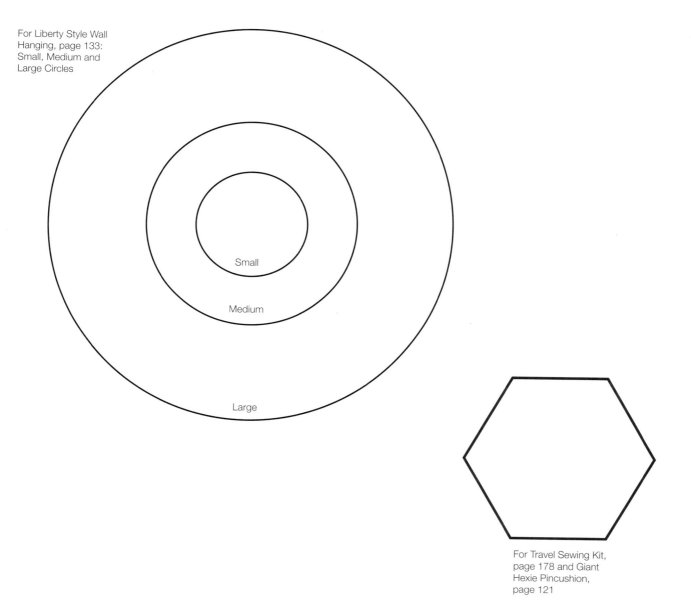

For Liberty Style Wall
Hanging, page 133:
Small, Medium and
Large Circles

Small

Medium

Large

For Travel Sewing Kit,
page 178 and Giant
Hexie Pincushion,
page 121

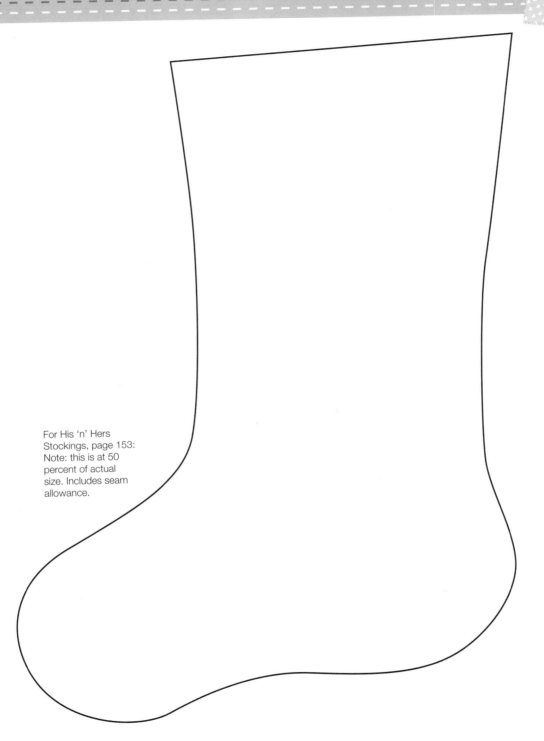

For His 'n' Hers
Stockings, page 153:
Note: this is at 50
percent of actual
size. Includes seam
allowance.

# Block Directory

# Block Directory

To make sure you have all the information you need to make these stunning quilts, here is a directory of blocks for your reference.

By switching colours or using a different stitching style, they form the basis of a large quilting repertoire. This section also includes variations and extensions of the major blocks, giving you even more ideas for beautiful quilts.

# Blocks with Squares and Rectangles

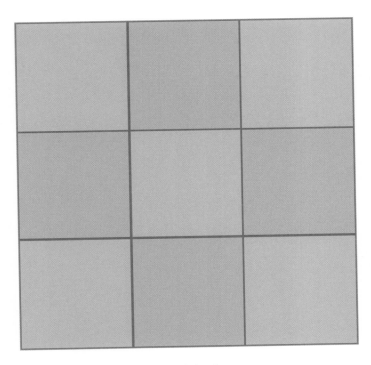

### Variations

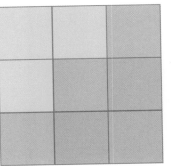

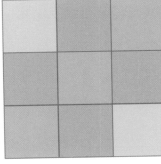

**Nine-Patch – 12 inches finished**

## Materials

Dark: 5 x (4½-inch) sqs
Light: 4 x (4½-inch) sqs

**1** Sew two rows of squares Dark/Light/Dark, and one row of Light/Dark/Light.

**2** Join rows following layout in the photograph.

## Variation:
### Disappearing Nine-Patch

Cut block in half horizontally then again vertically. Rearrange blocks as per photograph and sew back together as a four-patch.

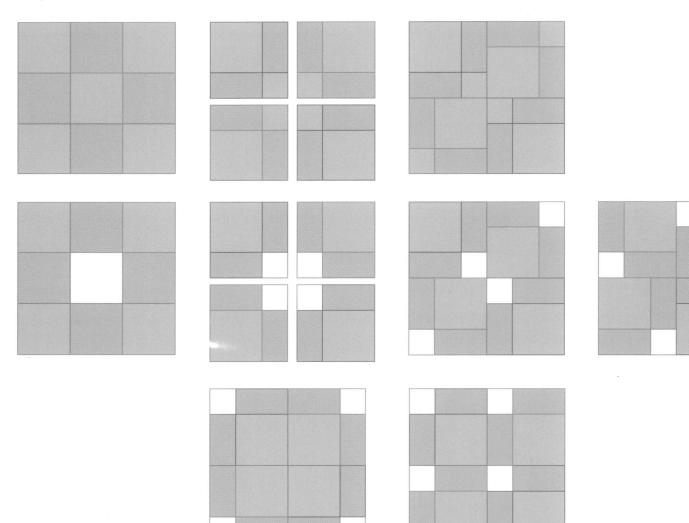

## Variation:
### Irish Chain

Start with 2½-inch squares. Once made up, pair nine
patches with 6½-inch light squares to create a single Irish
Chain quilt.

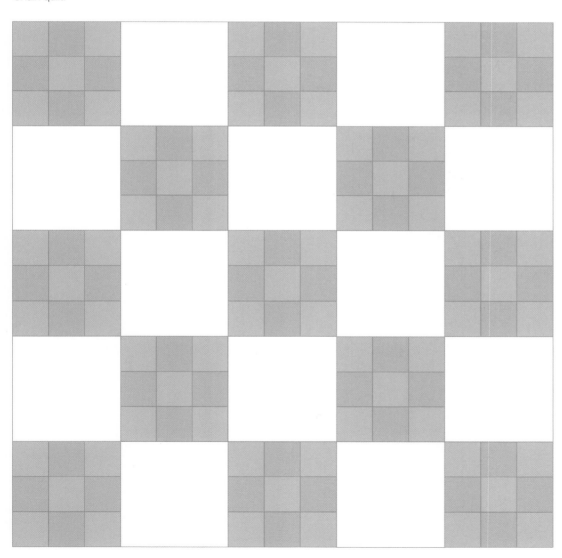

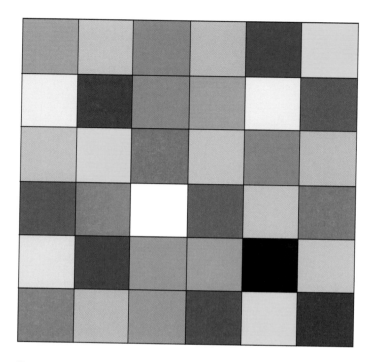

## Postage Stamp – 12 inches finished

### Materials
36 x (2½-inch) sqs

1 Arrange sqs in a six by six grid. Join into rows, then join rows to make the block. Take care to nest seams to reduce bulk.

Variations

## Chequerboard
Use 18 of each dark and light to create a chequerboard block.

## Trip Around the World
Arrange coloured squares diagonally as per photograph to create a trip around the world quilt; there are so many options for layouts with these quilts. Star, zigzag, trip, x and o, and radiating o – to name a few.

The Baby Steps Quilt on page 128 is an example of a postage stamp design.

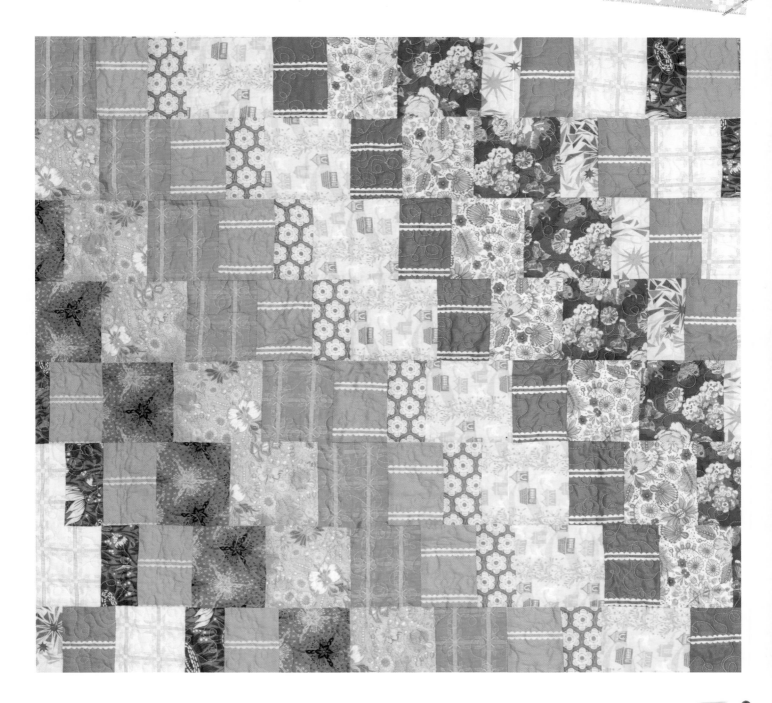

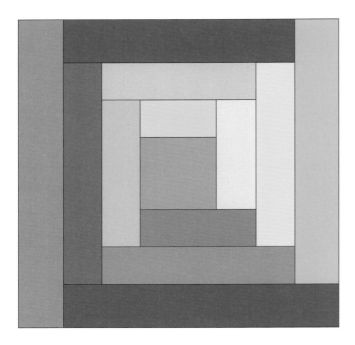

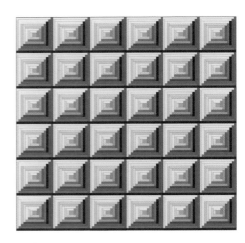

**Straight Setting**

## Log Cabin – 12 inches finished

### Materials

Centre: 3½ inches sq
Strips 2 inches wide, cut at the following lengths:
Light: 3½ inches, 5 inches, 6½ inches, 8 inches, 9½ inches, 11 inches
Dark: 5 inches, 6½ inches, 8 inches, 9½ inches, 11 inches, 12½ inches

1 Take the centre sq and two shortest light strips. Join the shortest light strip to the top of the square, press seam away from the centre. Join the second light strip to the RHS of the unit. Press seam away from the centre.

2 Take the two shortest dark strips. Attach the shortest dark strip to the bottom of the unit, and press seam away from the centre. Join the second dark strip to the LHS of the unit. Press seam away from the centre.

3 Repeat with the second and third round of logs, each time making sure the centre square is located with the shortest strip on top before you begin sewing to ensure you always begin in the same place.

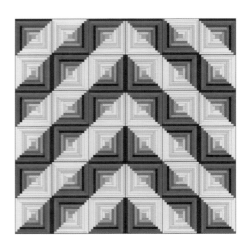

**Chevron**

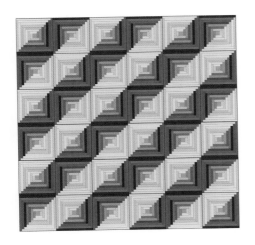

**Straight Furrows**

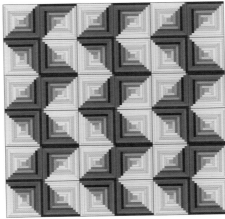

**Zigzag or Streaks of Lightning**

**Barn Raising**

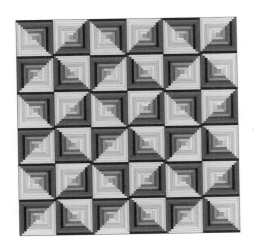

**Pinwheels**

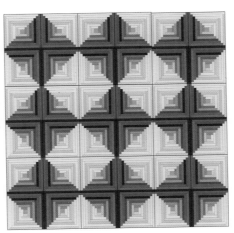

**Sunshine and Shadows**

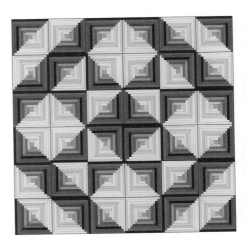

**Log Cabin Star**

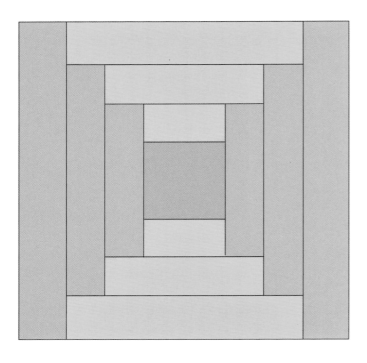

## Courthouse Steps – 12 inches finished

### Materials

Centre: 3½ inches sq
Strips 2 inches wide, cut at the following lengths:
Light: 2 x (3½ inches), 2 x (6½ inches), 2 x (9½ inches)
Dark: 2 x (6½ inches), 2 x (9½ inches), 2 x (12½ inches)

**1** Sew the two shortest light strips to top and bottom of centre square. Press seams away from the centre.

**2** Sew the two shortest dark strips to the RHS and LHS of the centre square. Press seams away from the centre.

**3** Repeat for second and third ring of logs, always beginning with the light strips.

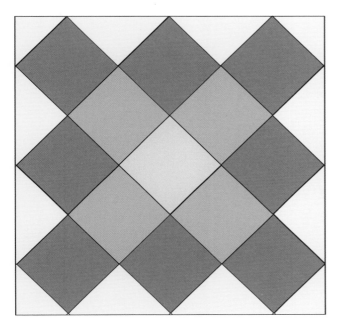

## Granny Square – 8½ inches finished

### Materials

25 x (2½-inch) sqs in the following colour groups:

Centre: 1

First round: 4

Second round: 8

BKG: 12

1 Arrange square following the layout in the diagram. The piecing for this block is done diagonally, or on-point. Starting with the first row, piece blocks together pressing seams alternately away or towards the centre.

2 Join rows together, nesting seams.

3 Join remaining two BKG squares to opposite edges.

4 Trim block to 9 inches square by aligning the ¼-inch mark on your ruler with the square points.

### Extension

Make a giant granny square by swapping the BKG squares for another colour, and adding 16 new BKG squares in the same manner.

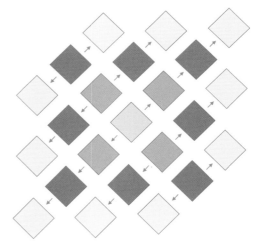

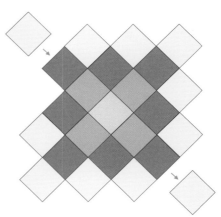

## Blocks with Half-Square Triangles

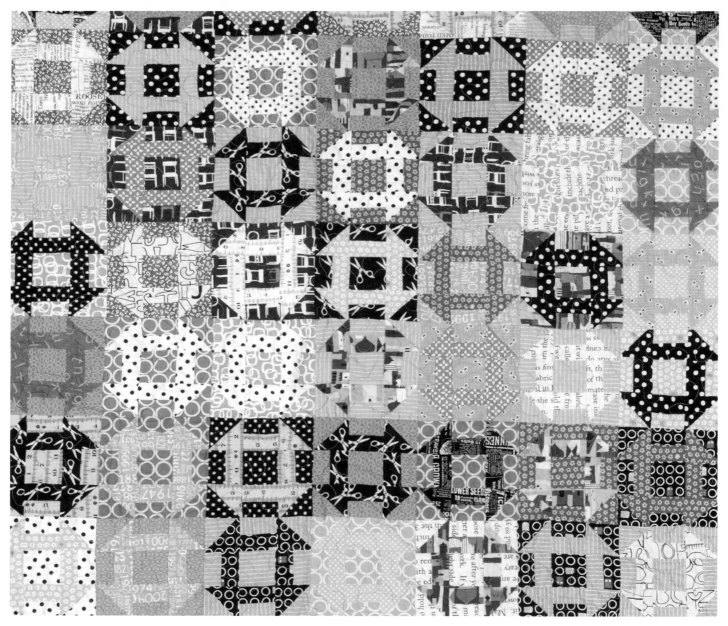

## Churn Dash – 12 inches finished

### Materials
Col A: 2 x (5-inch) sqs, 4 x (2½ x 4½-inch) rects
BKG: 2 x (5-inch) sqs, 4 x (2½ x 4½-inch) rects, 4½-inch sq

1 Pair 5-inch A and BKG sqs. Join to make HSTs. Trim to 4½ inches.

2 Pair A and BKG rects, join to make a square.

3 Arrange units following the layout in the photograph. Join as a four-patch.

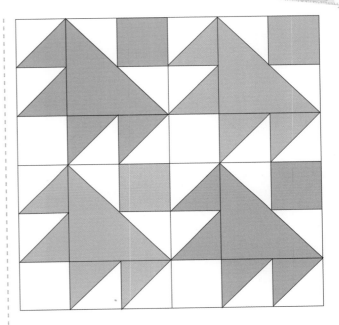

## Darting Birds – 9 inches finished

### Materials
Col A: 2½-inch small sq, 2 x (3-inch) medium sqs, 4⅞-inch large sq
BKG: 2½-inch small sq, 3 x (3-inch) medium sqs

1 Cut one of the 3-inch A sqs in half along the diagonal.

2 Pair remaining 3-inch A and BKG sqs. Join to make HSTs. Trim to 2½ inches.

3 Sew triangles made in step one to adjacent sides of A small sq to make large triangle.

4 Cut large A sq in half along the diagonal. Pair one half with large triangle created in step three. Sew together with a ¼-inch seam allowance.

5 Join HSTs together then piece the block as a four-patch following the layout in the photograph.

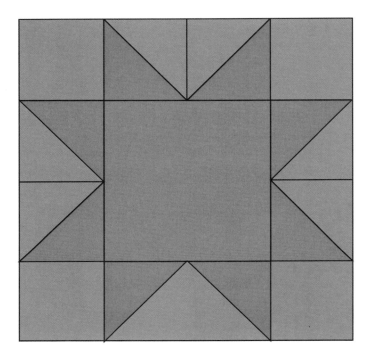

**Sawtooth Star – 12 inches finished**

## Materials

Col A: 6½-inch sq
Col B: 4 x (4-inch) sqs
BKG: 4 x (4-inch) sqs, 4 x (3½-inch) sqs

1 Pair 4 inch B and BKG sqs. Join to make HSTs. Trim to
3½ inches.

2 Arrange following the layout in the photograph. Join as a
nine-patch.

Extension:
Make a smaller sawtooth star to use as the centre 6½-inch block
using the following measurements and trimming HSTs to 2 inches:
Col A: 3½ inches sq
Col B: 4 x (2¾-inch) sqs
BKG: 4 x (2¾-inch) sqs, 4 x (2-inch) sqs

## Ribbon Star – 12 inches finished

### Materials

Col A: 6 x (4-inch) large sqs
BKG: 4 x (3½-inch) small sqs, 6 x (4-inch) large sqs

1 Pair large A and BKG sqs. Join to make HSTs.
  Trim to 3½-inch sqs.

2 Lay squares in a 16-patch with small BKG squares in
  outer corners.

3 Join as a 16-patch following the layout in the photograph.

## Dutchman's Puzzle – 12 inches finished

### Materials

Col A: 8 x (3½ x 6½-inch) rects
BKG: 16 x (3½-inch) sqs

1 Draw a diagonal line on the reverse of each BKG sq.

2 Place RST on one side of each rectangle, and sew along the line.
  Flip and press up to meet the top corner.

3 Flip back again and trim seam allowance to ¼ inch from the
  sewn line.

4 Repeat with second corner of each rectangle.

5 Sew geese into pairs, one on top of the other.

6 Arrange pairs in four-patch and sew together following the layout in
  the photograph.

## Other Blocks

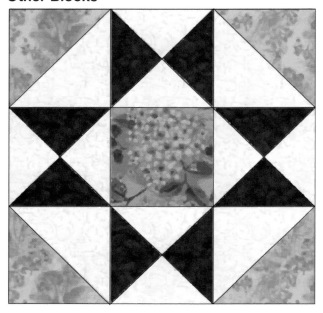

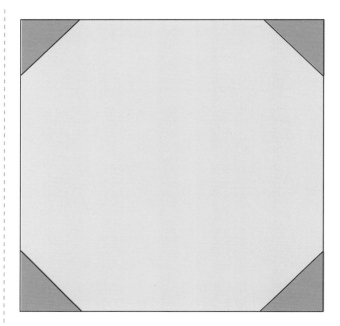

### Ohio Star – 12 inches finished

#### Materials

Block corners: 2 x (5-inch) sqs
Star points: 2 x (5¼-inch) sqs
Star centre: 4½-inch sq
BKG: 2 x (5-inch) small sqs, 2 x (5¼-inch) large sqs

1 Pair small corner and BKG squares. Join to make HSTs. Trim to 4½ inches.

2 Pair large point and BKG sqs. Join to make HSTs. Do not trim; pair again to make CSTs. Trim to 4½ inches.

3 Arrange as a nine-patch and sew together, following the layout in the diagram.

### Snowball – 9 inches finished

#### Materials

Col A: 9-inch sq
BKG: 4 x (3½ -inch) sqs

1 Draw a diagonal line on the reverse of each BKG sq.

2 Place RST on top of A square and sew along the line. Flip and press up to meet the top corner.

3 Flip back again and trim seam allowance to ¼ inch from the sewn line.

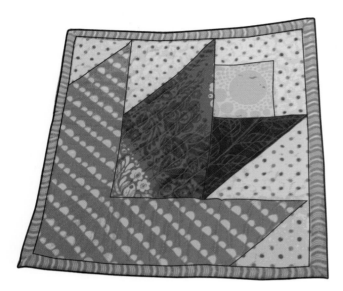

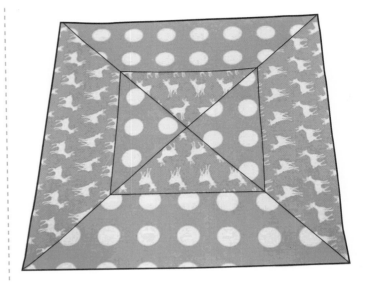

## Tulip – 9 inches finished

### Materials

Col A: Yellow; 2½ inches sq
Col B: Dark purple; 4 inches sq
Col C: Light purple; 3½ x 6½-inch rect
Col D: Green; 2½ x 6½-inch rect, 2½ x 8½-inch rect
BKG: 2 x (2½-inch) sqs, 3½-inch sq, 4-inch sq, 1½ x 2½-inch small rect, 1½ x 3½-inch large rect

1 Join A and small BKG rect. Sew large BKG rect to top of this unit.

2 Pair B and 4 inch BKG sqs. Join to make HSTs. Trim to 3½ inches. Join to bottom of step one unit.

3 Add 3½-inch BKG sqs as CST to C rect. Join to RHS of step two unit.

4 Add 2½-inch BKG sqs as CSTs to both D rects. Join short rect to bottom of step three unit, followed by longer rect to LHS.

## Double Hour Glass – 8 inches finished

### Materials (Makes two blocks)

Col A: 2½ inches x WOF strip
Col B: 2½ inches x WOF strip

1 Join strips along the length, being careful not to stretch or distort fabric. Press seam to darker fabric.

2 Cut off one end of the strip at a 45-degree angle. Using a large square ruler, position on-point so that the point of the square is at the top of the strip set and the left hand side aligns with the cut edge. Cut to form a triangle.

3 Reposition ruler so that the bottom point aligns with the bottom of the strip set. Cut to form another triangle. Repeat down the length of the strip to yield eight triangles.

4 Pair triangles with contrasting centre colours and join along one side to make half a square. Join two sets of pairs to make a square. Repeat to make second block.

5 Trim to 8 inches square.

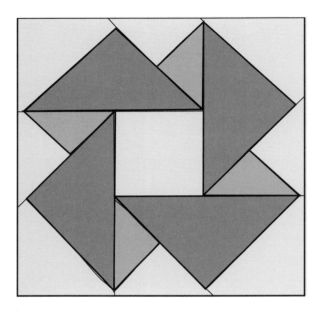

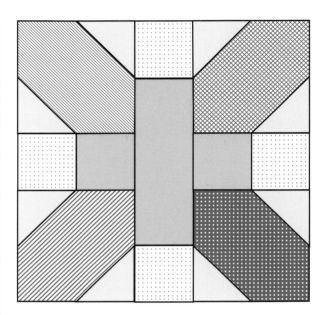

## Night Vision – 9 inches finished

### Materials
Centre: 3½ inches sq
Large points: 7¼ inches sq
Small points: 4¼ inches sq
BKG: 2 x (3⅞-inch) small sqs, 4¼-inch large sq

1 Cut large and small point sqs diagonally twice to create 4 triangles.

2 Cut small BKG sqs in half once, and large sq in half twice diagonally to create four triangles each.

3 Join one BKG and small point triangles on one short edge to create larger triangle.

4 Add unit made in step three as CST to RHS of large point triangle.

5 Add remaining BKG triangles as CST to LHS of large point triangle.

6 Sew blocks around centre sq using partial seams as described in technique section.

## + & X block – 8 inches finished

### Materials
X points: 4 x (3½-inch) sqs
Corners: 8 x (2-inch) sqs
Body: 2 x (2-inch) sqs, 2 x 5-inch rect
BKG: 4 x (2-inch) sqs

1 Draw a diagonal line on the reverse of each corner sq.

2 Add as CSTs to two opposite corners of each X point sq.

3 Join one BKG sq to either end of body rect.

4 Join remaining BKG sqs to body sqs.

5 Arrange and sew together in rows. Join rows to finish block.

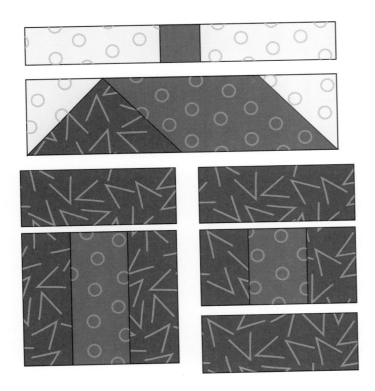

## House – 8 inches finished

### Materials

Sky: 2 x (1½ x 4-inch) rects, 2⅞ inches sq

Chimney: 1½ inches sq

Roof: 2½ x 7¼-inch rect

Gable: 5¼-inch sq

Door: 2⅞ x 4-inch rect

Window: 2⅞ x 2½-inch rect

Bricks: 2 x (1¾ x 2½-inch) small rects, 2 x (1¾ x 4¼-inch) medium rects, 3 x (2 x 4½-inch) large rects

1 Cut gable sq diagonally to form four triangles. Discard three. Cut sky sq in half to form two triangles. Cut two corners of roof rect at 45 degrees to form parallelogram.

2 Join roof to gable, then join sky triangles to either side to form row.

3 Join sky rects either side of chimney and sew to top of row formed in step two.

4 Join medium brick rects to either side of door. Add one large brick rect to top of unit.

5 Join small brick sqs to either side of window. Add one large brick rect to top and bottom of unit.

6 Join units made in step four and five, then join to roof unit.

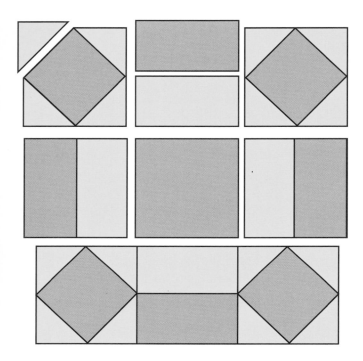

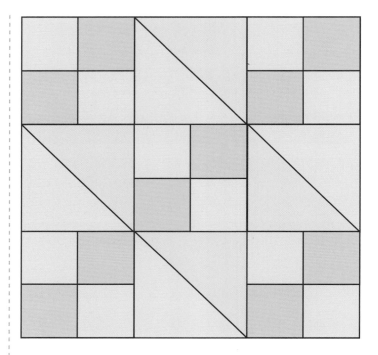

## Single Wedding Ring – 12 inches finished

### Materials

Col A: 4½-inch large sq, 4 x (2½ x 4½-inch) rects,
4 x (3⅛-inch) sml sqs
BKG: 8 x (2⅛-inch) sqs, 4 x (2½ x 4½-inch) rects

**1** Cut all BKG sqs in half along the diagonal to form 16 triangles.

**2** Add triangles to A small sqs as CSTs.

**3** Pair A/BKG rects and join.

**4** Join as a nine-patch following the layout in the photograph.

## Jacob's Ladder – 12 inches finished

### Materials

Col A (red): 2 x (5-inch) sqs, 10 x (2½-inch) sqs
Col B (blue): 2 x (5-inch) sqs
Col C (cream floral): 10 x (2½-inch) sqs

**1** Make 4 HSTs pairing A/BKG 5-inch sq. Trim to 4½ inches sq.

**2** Make five four-patches using the 2½-inch sqs.

**3** Assemble the block following the layout in the photograph.

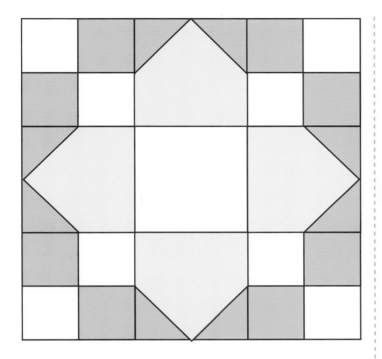

## Weather Vane

### Materials

Col A (red): 2 x (5-inch) sqs, 10 x (2½-inch) sqs
Col B (blue): 2 x (5-inch) sqs
Col C (cream floral): 10 x (2½-inch) sqs

**1** Add CSTs to 2 adjacent corners of each of the four medium 4½-inch sqs using light 2½-inch sqs.

**2** Sew two of those to either side of the light 4½-inch sq.

**3** Sew together eight pairs of dark and light 2½-inch sqs.

**4** Sew those into four four-patches.

**5** Sew block together using layout in the photograph.

## Prairie Flower

### Materials

Col A (white): 5 x (4½-inch) sqs
Col B (pink): 4 x (4½-inch) sqs
Col C (dark teal): 8 x (2½-inch) sqs
Col D (light teal): 8 x (2½-inch) sqs

**1** To each A sq, add two C sqs as CSTs to diagonally opposite corners to make block corner sqs.

**2** To each B sq, add two D sqs as CSTs to both top corners.

**3** Arrange and sew as nine-patch using photograph for reference.

## Dresden Plate – 15 inches finished

### Materials
BKG: 15½ inches sq
Petals: 16 x (4 x 6-inch) rects
Centre: 5 inches sq

1 Using template on page 187, cut 16 petals from assorted colours.

2 Fold petals in half along the length, RST, and sew a ¼-inch seam along the top edge. Clip corner at the fold edge to reduce bulk when folded. Press at this folded stage to create a crease down the centre of the leaf.

3 Turn dresden leaves through the right way and press the seam open using the tip of your iron. Use a turning tool or the tip of a pair of scissors to poke out the point when pressed.

4 Centre the seam on the centre crease as created in step two, and press to create the pointed edge.

5 Arrange in four groups of 16 leaves. Join 16 leaves together to make a circle. Press all seams in same direction so that they spiral around.

6 Cut a 3-inch circle from centre fabric and appliqué on to dresden centre using your favourite technique.

7 Appliqué dresden on to BKG sq using your chosen technique.

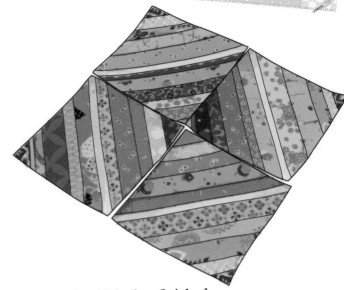

## String Block – 12 inches finished

### Materials
4 x (6½-inch) sqs of plain paper
White: 4 x (1 x 10-inch) strips
Assorted scraps: strips varying in width from 1–2½ inches

1 Turn stitch length down to approximately 1.5.

2 Centre white strip along diagonal, pin, or use small dab of glue stick to keep in place.

3 Place first strip RST with white strip and sew using a ¼-inch seam. Use dry iron to press outwards from centre.

4 Continue using stitch and flip technique until the whole side is covered, then repeat on the other side.

5 Turn over so paper side is showing; use paper to square up block to 6½ inches.

6 Repeat for further three blocks then remove paper by tearing along seam lines.

7 Join blocks in a four-patch as per photograph.

# Information

# Suppliers

Part of the fun of quilting is being creative with fabrics and materials. Although what you choose to use is entirely up to you, sometimes it's helpful to know which suppliers are tried-and-tested. These are the manufacturers and suppliers I recommend for quilting.

## Manufacturers

**Art Gallery Fabrics**
http://www.artgalleryquilts.com/

**Free Spirit**
http://www.freespiritfabric.com/

**Liberty**
http://www.liberty.co.uk/

**Michael Miller**
http://www.michaelmillerfabrics.com/

**Moda**
http://www.unitednotions.com/

**Riley Blake**
http://www.rileyblakedesigns.com/

**Robert Kaufman**
http://www.robertkaufman.com/

**Timeless Treasures**
http://www.ttfabrics.com/

**Windham Fabrics**
http://www.windhamfabrics.com/

## Suppliers

**Fat Quarter Shop**
http://www.fatquartershop.com/

**Fabric**
http://www.fabric.com

**Keepsake Quilting**
http://www.keepsakequilting.com

**Quilting Fabric Supplier**
http://www.quiltingfabricsupplier.com

**Pink Castle Fabrics**
http://www.pinkcastlefabrics.com

**Simply Solids**
http://simplysolids.co.uk/

**Sew Me a Song**
http://www.etsy.com/shop/sewmeasong

**The Organic Stitch Co**
http://www.etsy.com/shop/GreeneStitchCo

**Quilting Warehouse**
http://www.quilting-warehouse.com

# Glossary of Quilting Terms

**Four-Patch** Quilt block made up of four squares in a two by two layout. Also used as a method of construction.

**Nine-patch** Quilt block made up of nine squares in a three by three layout. Also used as a method of construction.

**16-Patch** Quilt block made up of 16 squares in a four by four layout. Also used as a method of construction.

**Appliqué** Decorative piece of fabric applied on top of a background using hand or machine stitching.

**Appliqué Pins** Short and sharp pins used for securing intricate shapes to the background fabric in preparation for hand stitching. Appliqué glue can also be used.

**Backing** Large piece of fabric used for the back of a quilt. Often pieced from two lengths to achieve desired width.

**Bar Tack** Thick rectangle of stitching repeated over itself, usually with a zigzag stitch and often in conjunction with inserting a zip.

**Basting** Process of temporarily securing the 3 layers of quilt fabric together in preparation for quilting.

**Batting** The middle layer of the quilt sandwich which gives the quilt a padded look. Can be made from cotton, silk, polyester, wool or other synthetic materials, also known as wadding/padding.

**Betweens** Short thin needles used for quilting.

**Bias** Diagonal grain of a fabric. Fabric that is cut at 45 degrees to the selvedge has the most stretch and is suitable for binding circular objects.

**Binding** Strips of fabric used to encase raw edges of a project. Can be double fold (as in a quilt) or single fold (as in small projects or clothing).

**Block** Single pieced section of a quilt. One block can be repeated for a whole quilt, or many blocks of different designs can be used to create a sampler style quilt. Blocks are sewn together, with or without sashing, to create the quilt top.

**Border** Frame applied to a block or quilt as a whole. Used to increase the size of a quilt or as a design element.

**Chain Piecing** Process of sewing patches of fabric together without stopping between each one. Threads are clipped after all pieces are sewn. This saves time and thread.

**Charm Pack** Selection of 5-inch squares of fabric.

**Cornerstones** Small squares of fabric used in the joins between blocks and sashing.

**Ditch** Slight indentation between two patchwork pieces. Stitch-in-the-ditch is the process of quilting along this line; adding quilting and design to the back of the quilt which will be mostly hidden on the front.

**Echo Quilting** Process of quilting around a shape, echoing or replicating its design outwards, much like a raindrop into a puddle.

**Finger Press** Process of applying pressure to a seam line using finger and thumb, without using an iron.

**Flying Geese** Patchwork unit consisting of a large triangle, with smaller triangles either side making it into a rectangle.

**Fat Quarter** A true quarter of a yard of fabric measuring 18 x 22 inches.

**Freezer Paper** Paper with a waxed side, useful for appliqué projects, making templates and temporary stiffening.

**Fussy Cut** Process of cutting shapes from fabric to make the most of the design, or to cut all pieces for a block with the same pattern on.

**Fusible Web** Synthetic material made from a web of fibres that will fuse to fabric when heat and pressure is applied. Usually used for stiffening or appliqué projects.

**Grain** The direction the threads run in a fabric. The horizontal thread is known as the crossways grain, the vertical is known as the lengthways grain, and the diagonal is known as the bias.

**Jelly Roll** Selection of 2 ½ inches x WOF strips of fabric.

**Layer Cake** Selection of 10-inch squares of fabric.

**Layout** Process of auditioning positions for blocks in a quilt to make the most favourable balance of colour and shapes.

**Log Cabin** Traditional quilt block made by sewing strips of varying length around a centre square.

**Marking** Process of applying temporary guidelines to a quilt top in preparation for quilting.

**Mitre** Style of border and binding finish for quilts where two fabrics meet at a 45-degree angle.

**Orphan Block** Leftover quilt block/s from a finished project. Can be used singularly to make small items such as potholders, placemats, etc., pieced into a larger improvised project, or used on the back of a quilt.

**Patch** Small piece of fabric, usually combined with others to form a block.

**Pieced** Piece of fabric created by sewing patches together.

**Pressing** The action of applying heat to a piece of fabric in an up-and-down motion. Used to set seams.

**Quarter-Inch** The most important measurement in quilting. Nearly all block designs, tutorials and patterns are based around the elusive quarter-inch seam allowance. A good quarter-inch foot for your sewing machine is essential.

**QAYG** Quilt-as-you-go: the process of sewing fabric directly on to batting to create re-quilted blocks. Blocks are then sewn together and lightly quilted on to a backing. (See techniques on page 76.)

**Quilt Sandwich** The three layers of a quilt comprising of quilt top, batting and backing.

**Ric Rac** A woven trimming which looks like a rounded zigzag.

**Rotary Cutter** Handheld cutting device with a circular blade, used for cutting multiple layers of fabric at once.

**Sampler Quilt** Quilt made up of many different blocks, usually put together with sashing and cornerstones.

**Sashing** Long strips of fabric used to join blocks together when making a quilt.

**Scraps** Small pieces of fabric leftover from other projects which can be used to make scrap quilts.

**Seam Allowance** The specified amount of fabric from a patch which will be used for the seam.

**Selvedge** The finished edge of the fabric. Usually printed with fabric information such as manufacturer, designer and name of the print. Selvedges are often cut off and discarded, but due to their un-fraying nature they are great to use in small projects as trimming/decoration. (See stocking project on page 153.)

**Squaring Up** Process of trimming a piece of fabric to make it a true square. Marks on a cutting mat or a large square ruler can be used to achieve this.

**String** A long thin piece of fabric.

**Strip Piecing** Process of sewing long strips together, i.e. jelly roll strip. This is usually done as a time saving device for when the strips will be sub-cut and rearranged.

**Templates** A pattern piece, usually made from cardboard or plastic, used for tracing on to fabric before it is cut out.

**Tied** Quick method of permanently securing the three layers of a quilt together. Thread or yarn is stitched through the quilt sandwich and secured with a square knot.

**Value** How light or dark a fabric 'reads'. The actual colour of the fabric is not important here, just its brightness. A good way to test for this is to take a black and white or greyscale photograph of your project.

**Voile** Light and silky cotton fabric with a high thread count. Most often used in dressmaking, but makes very luxurious quilts.

**Y-Seams** Also known as inset seams, where three pieces of fabric come together to make a point. Most commonly found when working with diamonds.

**Yardage** The term quilters use to denote an amount of fabric, usually one yard or greater.

# Abbreviations

| | | | | |
|---|---|---|---|---|
| **BKG** | Background | | **QAYG** | Quilt as you go |
| **Col** | Colour | | **rect(s)** | Rectangle(s) |
| **CST** | Corner-square triangles | | **RHS** | Right hand side |
| **EPP** | English paper piecing | | **RS** | Right side(s) |
| **F8ths** | Fat eighths | | **RST** | Right sides together |
| **FQ** | Fat quarter | | **sml** | Small |
| **FPP** | Foundation paper piecing | | **sq(s)** | Square(s) |
| **FMQ** | Free motion quilting | | **WOF** | Width of fabric |
| **HST** | Half-square triangle | | **WS** | Wrong side(s) |
| **hex** | Hexagon | | **WSF** | Wrong side facing |
| **LHS** | Left hand side | | **WST** | Wrong sides together |
| **lrg** | Large | | **yd(s)** | Yard(s) |
| **LQS** | Local quilting store | | | |

# Index

Pages in **bold** refer to templates.

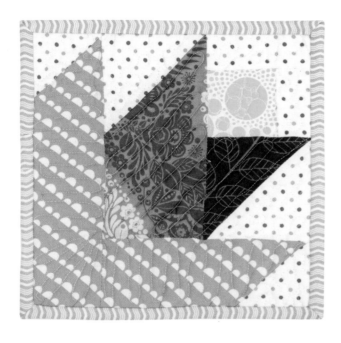

# Acknowledgements

Thank you to everyone at Quintet Publishing for offering me this opportunity; especially Caroline for your help and encouragement along the way.

To Karen, Martin, Simon and Paula, for your constant love and support in everything that I attempt. For convincing me that I can do anything I put my mind to, and for providing Sunday dinners when I'm up to my ears in fabric.

To Tash, and my extended family and friends for always being there as a sounding board and for being proud of me and my projects.

Thank you to the Kitchen Guild and Brit Bee girls; you are an endless source of inspiration and I'm so happy to call you my people.

Last but not least, to Warren. For being the best wingman a girl could ask for.

# Picture Credits

A = above, B = below, L = left, R = right, C = centre, T = top, F = far

**Alamy** 9 © The National Trust Photolibrary; 48 © Valery Voennyy; 219 © Jonathan Boshoff.

**Denyse Schmidt Quilts** 9.

**Getty** 99 © Sandy Jones.

**iStock** 14T, 18, 19, 20, 23, 29, 39TL, 85.

**Laura Jane Taylor** 8, 54T, 55T, 95L, 95R.

**Shutterstock** 15, 16, 22L, 22R, 28, 31, 32, 36, 37, 38C, 38BR, 38T, 38BL, 38CL, 39BL, 39CL, 39C, 39CR, 39 BR, 60L, 68, 82, 94R, 98T.

**Sussie Bell** 50, 89.